with

BTS

Global Edition

Contents

Structure and Features

Episode Intro

Kate's vlog thumbnail introduces the topic and learning objective.

Warm-up

Get a head start on your learning with BTS-related warm-up questions.

Vlog Intro

Check out Kate's vlog to get a preview of what you will learn in this chapter.

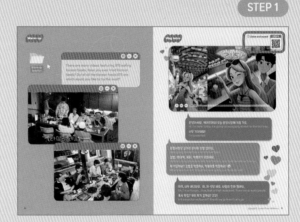

STEP 1

⊙ **Download the Cake app**

Use the Cake app with 〈EASY KOREAN with BTS〉!

STEP 1

⊙ Scan the QR code to listen to Kate's vlog. Listen and repeat.

STEP 2

⊙ Use the app to learn the vocabulary.

STEP 3

⊙ Get more practice with vocabulary quizzes.

Vocabulary

Learn the vocabulary
and answer simple practice questions.

STEP 2   STEP 3

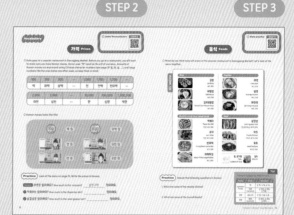

Expression

Learn expressions and solve
expression exercises.

◇ **EASY to Use!**
Learn expressions and find out
how to use them easily.

◇ **EASY to Speak!**
Read the main example sentences of
each expression aloud.

STEP 4, STEP 6   STEP 5, STEP 7

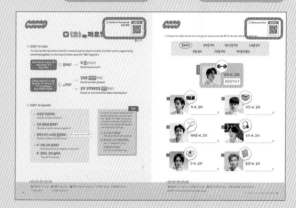

STEP 4, STEP 6

⊙ Listen to the Korean expression lecture.
You can watch ⟨Run BTS!⟩ videos as you
learn the expressions.

STEP 5, STEP 7

⊙ Get more practice with
expression quizzes.

STEP 8

⊙ Listen to Kate and Shun's
dialogue and repeat.

Dialogue

Learn through Kate and Shun's dialogue, which takes place in many different situations. Once you have mastered the dialogue, you can also try out the dialogue activities. (Dialogue translations are provided on page 174.)

(Dialogue translations are provided on page 174.)

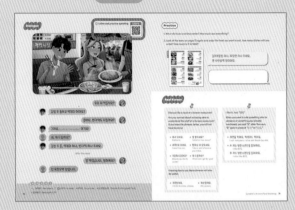

Real Korean

Learn Korean expressions that Koreans use frequently in real life.

BTS Time

Wrap up the chapter with BTS anecdotes that are related to the topic.

Create Your Own Vlog

Like Kate, make a vlog as you go over what you have learned in this chapter.

Use your Workbook to review what you have learned from the Student Book. You can also download the Workbook PDF file using the QR code.

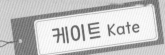
케이트 Kate

⭐ **Personality**
Bright and cheerful

⭐ **Hobbies**
Vlogging, dancing, and traveling

⭐ **My BTS Story** ♥

2017 Fell in love with BTS' awesome performance
in the "MIC Drop" video and became a fan

2019 Attended her first concert, "LOVE YOURSELF : SPEAK
YOURSELF"

2022 Uploaded her first BTS dance cover video on her channel

Currently Traveling in Korea to learn Korean and K-pop dance,
as well as to visit BTS-related spots

슌 Shun

⚙ **Personality**
Warm and calm

⚙ **Hobbies**
Cooking, singing, and traveling

⚙ **My BTS Story** ♥

2018 Fell in love with BTS' amazing song "FAKE LOVE" and became a fan

2019 Attended his first concert, "LOVE YOURSELF"

2021 〈IN THE SOOP BTS ver. Season 2〉 sparked his interest in Korean
food, which led to his first visit to Korea

Currently Traveling in Korea for a second time to learn Korean and
how to make Korean food, as well as to visit BTS-related spots

**Kate and Shun first meet in a Korean class in Korea.
As they travel around the country,
they have many fun experiences...**

Warm-up Question

BTS wrote in Hangeul.
What did they write?

〈Run BTS!〉 EP. 86 - 한글날 특집 1

한글 소개 About Hangeul

Have you seen the Hangeul Day episodes 86 and 87 on 〈Run BTS!〉? In honor of Hangeul Day, BTS took a quiz about Hangeul and played a game where they had to make Korean words with vowel and consonant puzzles. Hangeul Day commemorates the invention of Hangeul, the writing system of the Korean language. In 1443, King Sejong the Great invented Hangeul, allowing Koreans to read and write easily. Hangeul is easy for anyone to learn. So let's give it a try!

Hangeul is composed of vowels and consonants. The basic vowels are based on the shapes of a round sky (•), flat ground (—), and standing person (|). Additional vowels can be created by combining these letters together.

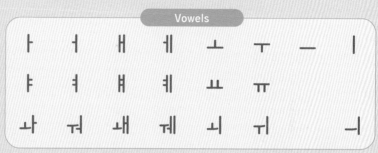

Vowels

ㅏ	ㅓ	ㅐ	ㅔ	ㅗ	ㅜ	ㅡ	ㅣ
ㅑ	ㅕ	ㅒ	ㅖ	ㅛ	ㅠ		
ㅘ	ㅝ	ㅙ	ㅞ	ㅚ	ㅟ		ㅢ

The consonants in Hangeul are based on the shape of the vocal organs. Strokes can be added and the same consonant can be written twice to create different sounding consonants.

Consonants

ㄱ	ㄴ	ㅁ	ㅅ	ㅇ
	ㄷ	ㅂ	ㅈ	
ㅋ	ㅌ	ㅍ	ㅊ	ㅎ
	ㄹ			
ㄲ	ㄸ	ㅃ	ㅆ ㅉ	

한글의 음절 Syllables in Hangeul

In Hangeul, vowels and consonants combine to form syllables. A syllable must have a vowel and can be preceded and followed by one consonant sound. There are four different syllable structures. When you write a syllable, you write the letters together inside a roughly square shape. The consonant that comes at the end of a syllable is called the "받침" (batchim), and it is always written at the bottom of the syllable.

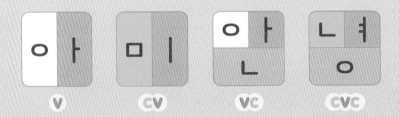

① V (vowel)

Only the vowel makes a sound. The "ㅇ" that comes first is silent and acts as a placeholder.

② C + V (consonant + vowel)

A consonant is placed before a vowel. The consonant and vowel come together to make a single sound.

③ V + C (vowel + consonant)

A vowel is followed by a consonant (batchim). (Here, if the consonant "ㅇ" is in the batchim, it has a sound.)

④ C + V + C (consonant + vowel + consonant)

Type the letters in the correct order on the Korean keyboard, and they will automatically form syllables.

First, try typing "아미 안녕." Find the consonants and vowels on your keyboard, and type them one by one in the order shown below. The syllables will form automatically.

1 아: ㅇ → ㅏ

2 미: ㅁ → ㅣ

3 안: ㅇ → ㅏ → ㄴ

4 녕: ㄴ → ㅕ → ㅇ

Practice

1. Let's say you typed the following on your Korean keyboard. Choose the correct syllables below.

ㄷ → ㅏ → ㄹ → ㄹ → ㅕ → ㄹ → ㅏ

1 다ㄹ려라 **2** 다ㄹ려라 **3** 달려라 **4** 달ㄹㅏ

2. You are trying to type the word "방탄." Write the consonants and vowels in the correct order in the blanks under the word, and write the numbers on the keys in the order you would press them on the keyboard.

방탄

ㅂ ☐ ☐ ☐ ☐ ☐

ㅇ ㅂ ㅌ
ㅏ ㅏ ㄴ

모음 1 Vowel 1

🔊 **Listen to the Hangeul audio and get more practice**

STEP 1-2

These are the simple vowels. Listen and repeat.

The vowels below are pronounced by opening your mouth wider in a downward motion.

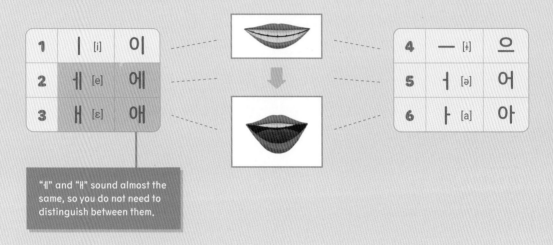

1	ㅣ [i] 이
2	ㅔ [e] 에
3	ㅐ [ɛ] 애

4	ㅡ [ɨ] 으
5	ㅓ [ə] 어
6	ㅏ [a] 아

"ㅔ" and "ㅐ" sound almost the same, so you do not need to distinguish between them.

The vowels below are pronounced by rounding the lips.

| 7 | ㅜ [u] 우 |
| 8 | ㅗ [o] 오 |

Practice Read the Hangeul and write it.

The shape of the vowel determines where you write it. "ㅏ, ㅓ, ㅐ, ㅔ, ㅣ" are written on the right side of the consonant, and "ㅗ, ㅜ, ㅡ" are written below the consonant.

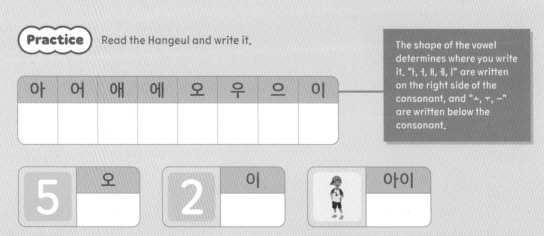

아	어	애	에	오	우	으	이

5	오

2	이

	아이

자음 1 Consonant 1

🔊 **Listen to the Hangeul audio and get more practice**

STEP 3-4

These are the basic consonants. They are pronounced from different places.
Listen and repeat.

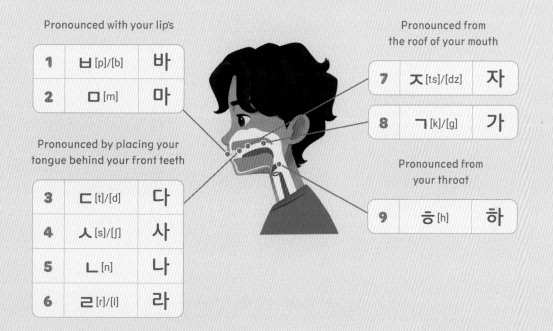

Pronounced with your lip's

1	ㅂ [p]/[b]	바
2	ㅁ [m]	마

Pronounced by placing your tongue behind your front teeth

3	ㄷ [t]/[d]	다
4	ㅅ [s]/[ʃ]	사
5	ㄴ [n]	나
6	ㄹ [r]/[l]	라

Pronounced from the roof of your mouth

7	ㅈ [ts]/[dz]	자
8	ㄱ [k]/[g]	가

Pronounced from your throat

9	ㅎ [h]	하

Practice   Read the Hangeul and write it.

바	마	다	사	나	라	자	가	하

보	모	도	소	노	로	조	고	호

가수

나비

모자

하루

모음 2 Vowel 2

🔊 **Listen to the Hangeul audio and get more practice**

These are vowels made by modifying the simple vowels you learned on page 12.
Listen and repeat.

Add a stroke to the vowels. Make a short /y/ sound,
and then immediately pronounce the following vowel.

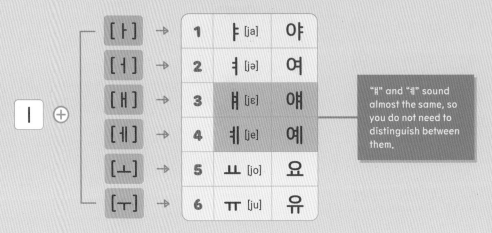

[ㅏ] →	1	ㅑ [ja]	야
[ㅓ] →	2	ㅕ [jə]	여
[ㅐ] →	3	ㅒ [jɛ]	얘
[ㅔ] →	4	ㅖ [je]	예
[ㅗ] →	5	ㅛ [jo]	요
[ㅜ] →	6	ㅠ [ju]	유

ㅣ ⊕

"ㅒ" and "ㅖ" sound almost the same, so you do not need to distinguish between them.

Add "ㅗ" or "ㅜ" to the vowels. Make a short /w/ sound,
and then immediately pronounce the following vowel.

[ㅏ] →	7	ㅘ [wa]	와
[ㅓ] →	8	ㅝ [wə]	워
[ㅐ] →	9	ㅙ [wɛ]	왜
[ㅔ] →	10	ㅞ [we]	웨
[ㅣ] →	11	ㅚ [we]	외
[ㅣ] →	12	ㅟ [wi]	위

ㅗ, ㅜ ⊕

"ㅙ," "ㅞ," and "ㅚ" sound almost the same, so you do not need to distinguish between them.

"ㅢ" is pronounced by adding the "ㅣ" sound after "ㅡ."

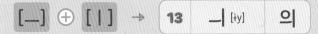

[ㅡ] ⊕ [ㅣ] → | 13 | ㅢ [ɨy] | 의

야	여	얘	예	요	유

와	워	왜	웨	외	위		의

 야구

 얘기

 요리

 우유

 와

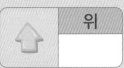 위

 야외

 의사

자음 2 Consonant 2

🎧 **Listen to the Hangeul audio and get more practice** **STEP 7-8**

These are consonants made by adding strokes or repeating the basic consonants you learned on page 13. Listen and repeat.

Pronounce these with a strong burst of air.

❶ ㅂ [p]/[b]	❹ ㄷ [t]/[d]	❼ ㅅ [s]/[ʃ]	❾ ㅈ [ts]/[dz]	❿ ㄱ [k]/[g]
바	다	사	자	가
❷ ㅍ [pʰ]	❺ ㅌ [tʰ]		❿ ㅊ [tsʰ]	❸ ㅋ [kʰ]
파	타		차	카
❸ ㅃ [p']	❻ ㄸ [t']	❽ ㅆ [s']/[ʃ']	⓫ ㅉ [ts']	⓮ ㄲ [k']
빠	따	싸	짜	까

Pronounce strongly from your throat without releasing a burst of air from your mouth.

Practice Read the Hangeul and write it.

바	파	빠

다	타	따

사	싸

자	차	짜

가	카	까

	토끼

	차

	쓰다

	커피

	오빠

again	또

받침 Batchim

Many consonants can be a batchim, but they are pronounced as only one of the following seven sounds. Listen and repeat.

> Sometimes two different consonants make up a batchim, but only one of them is pronounced.

Main Pronunciations

① ㄴ [n]

ㄴ		ㄵ	ㄶ
눈 eye; snow	산 mountain	앉다 to sit	많다 to be a lot

② ㄹ [l]

ㄹ	ㄼ	ㄾ	ㅀ
불 fire	여덟 eight	핥다 to lick	싫다 to dislike

③ ㅁ [m]

ㅁ		ㄻ
몸 body	사람 person	삶 life

④ ㅇ [ŋ]

ㅇ	
공 ball	사랑 love

⑤ ㅂ [p]

ㅂ	ㅍ	ㅄ	ㄿ
지갑 wallet	숲 forest	없다 to not exist	읊다 to recite

⑥ ㄷ [t]

ㄷ	ㅌ	ㅅ	ㅆ	ㅈ	ㅊ
곧 soon	끝 end	옷 clothes	있다 to exist	낮 daytime	꽃 flower

⑦ ㄱ [k]

ㄱ	ㅋ	ㄲ	ㄳ	ㄺ
책 book	부엌 kitchen	낚시 fishing	몫 share, portion	읽다 to read

한글 연습 Hangeul Practice

When writing syllables, write the initial consonant, vowel, and batchim one letter at a time.
As for the strokes, write from left to right and top to bottom.

Practice These are the titles of BTS songs. Think about which songs they are as you trace them.

피	땀	눈	물
피	땀	눈	물

아	이	돌
아	이	돌

봄	날
봄	날

소	우	주
소	우	주

온
온

다	이	너	마	이	트
다	이	너	마	이	트

달	려	라	방	탄
달	려	라	방	탄

Practice The following are BTS' real names. Read the Hangeul and complete the name tag under each photo.

김 남 준   김 석 진   민 윤 기

정 호 석   박 지 민   김 태 형   전 정 국

기본 발음 규칙 Linking Sounds

When reading Hangeul, the sounds of individual letters may change slightly to make it easier to pronounce. First, when a batchim is followed by a vowel, the batchim replaces "ㅇ" of the next syllable.

한국어	작은 것들을 위한 시
[한구거]	[자근 걷드를 위한 시]

눈을 감아	꽃이 떨어져요
[누늘 가마]	[꼬치 떠러저요]

If the batchim is made up of two different consonants, such as "ㄵ," "ㄻ," "ㄺ," only the last consonant replaces the "ㅇ" of the next syllable.

앉아요	읽어요
[안자요]	[일거요]

Batchim "ㅎ" is silent when followed by a vowel.

좋아요	넣어요
[조아요]	[너어요]

When the sounds of the consonants "ㄱ," "ㄷ," "ㅂ," "ㅈ," meet "ㅎ," the two sounds are combined and they become "ㅋ," "ㅌ," "ㅍ" and "ㅊ."

ㄱ + ㅎ → ㅋ	ㅎ + ㄷ → ㅌ
축하해	좋다
[추카해]	[조타]

ㅂ + ㅎ → ㅍ	ㅎ + ㅈ → ㅊ
복잡해진 맘	많지 않지
[복자패진 맘]	[만치 안치]

Episode 1

한국어로 자기소개하기

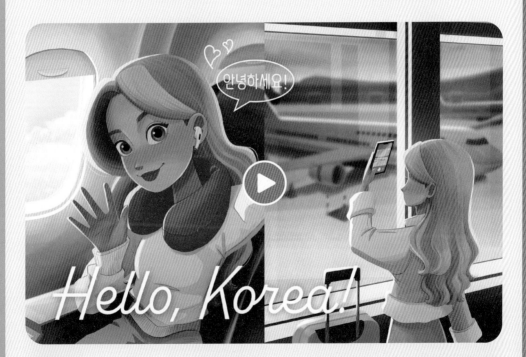

INTRODUCE YOURSELF IN KOREAN | KOREA VLOG

안녕하세요!

Hello, Korea!

 KATE

Learning Objective

#Introduce_Yourself   #Introduce_Someone   #Nice_to_Meet_You

Warm-up

Warm-up
Question

Imagine you are in Korea and you meet BTS one day.
If you had to introduce yourself to BTS,
what would you say?

안녕하세요. 반가워요! 😊 저는 케이트예요.
Hello. Nice to meet you! I'm Kate.

여기는 한국이에요. 저는 미국에서 왔어요.
This is South Korea. I'm from the United States.
저는 방탄소년단 팬이에요.
I'm a fan of BTS.

앞으로 잘 부탁드립니다. 그럼 안녕!
I hope to see you again. Bye!

Vocabulary

나라와 지역 Countries and Regions

⟡ Kate is from the United States. How do you say the names of countries and regions in Korean?

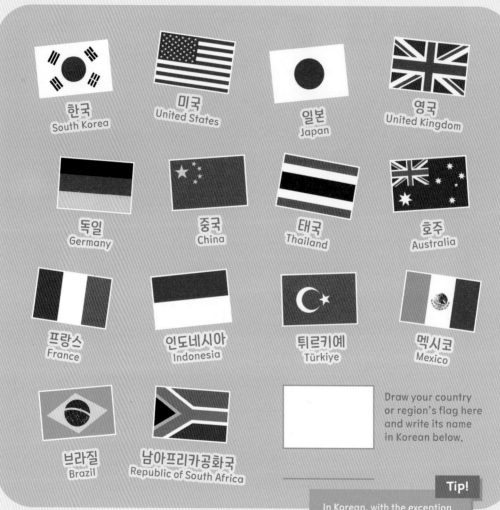

한국
South Korea

미국
United States

일본
Japan

영국
United Kingdom

독일
Germany

중국
China

태국
Thailand

호주
Australia

프랑스
France

인도네시아
Indonesia

튀르키예
Türkiye

멕시코
Mexico

브라질
Brazil

남아프리카공화국
Republic of South Africa

Draw your country or region's flag here and write its name in Korean below.

_____

Tip!

In Korean, with the exception of "미국, 일본, 영국, 독일, 중국, 태국, 호주, etc.," country and region names are usually written to reflect the pronunciation in either the country or region's language or English.

Practice Where are you from?

→ 저는 _____ 에서 왔어요.

이, 그, 저

⬦ Kate used "여기" to refer to the place where she was. "이, 그, 저" can be used to refer to things, people, places, etc. Depending on the location, "이, 그, 저" are used differently.

Ⓝ noun

	이 Ⓝ (close to the speaker)	그 Ⓝ (far from the speaker and close to the listener)	저 Ⓝ (far from both the speaker and the listener)
Object	이 의자 this chair	그 의자 that chair	저 의자 that chair
Person	이 사람 this person 이 분 (honorific)	그 사람 that person 그 분 (honorific)	저 사람 that person 저 분 (honorific)

Pronoun (spoken Korean)	이거 this	그거 that	저거 that
Direction	이쪽 this way	그쪽 that way	저쪽 that way
Place	여기 here	거기 there	저기 there

(**Practice**) Circle the word that matches the context of the pictures.

1

여기   거기   저기

2

이거   그거   저거

3

이 사람   그 사람   저 사람

N¹은/는 N²이에요/예요

N noun

✧ EASY to Use!

You can use this expression when you are introducing someone or something. "N¹은/는" refers to the person or thing that you are describing, and "N²이에요/예요" refers to the description of the person or thing. You can omit "N¹은/는" when it is clear who or what you are describing.

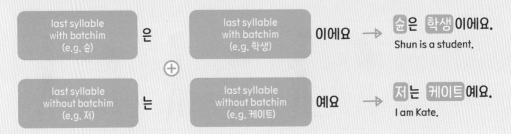

| last syllable with batchim (e.g. 숨) | 은 | last syllable with batchim (e.g. 학생) | 이에요 | → | 숨은 학생이에요. Shun is a student. |

⊕

| last syllable without batchim (e.g. 저) | 는 | last syllable without batchim (e.g. 케이트) | 예요 | → | 저는 케이트예요. I am Kate. |

✧ EASY to Speak!

- 이 사람은 제 친구예요.
  This person is my friend.

- 제 친구는 일본 사람이에요.
  My friend is Japanese.

- 여기는 한국이에요.
  This is Korea.

- A : 이름이 뭐예요?
  What is your name?
- B : 숨이에요.
  It is Shun.

Tip!

This expression can be used to say your name, country or region of origin, profession, etc.

A : 직업이 뭐예요? (= 무슨 일 해요?)
  What is your job? (= What do you do?)
B : 가수예요.
  I am a singer.

It can also be used to say that you are a fan of a particular artist.

저는 방탄소년단 팬이에요. 😊
I am a fan of BTS.

N 학생 student N 저 I, me N 사람 person • 제 my N 친구 friend N 이름 name N 뭐 what
N 직업 job • 무슨 일 해요? What do you do? N 가수 singer N 방탄소년단 BTS N 팬 fan

Practice

1. Complete the sentences by choosing the correct expressions.

❶ 저 은 / 는 아미 이에요 / 예요 .   ❷ 우리 은 / 는 친구 이에요 / 예요 .

❸ 이 분 은 / 는 선생님 이에요 / 예요 .   ❹ 저 사람 은 / 는 누구 이에요 / 예요 ?

2. Complete the sentences using the given words.

케이트

저는 케이트예요.

1
한국 사람

저는 _____ .

2
의사

저는 _____ .

3
방탄소년단

우리는 _____ .

4
?
your name

저는 _____ .

ᴠᵒᶜᵃᵇᵘˡᵃʳʸ

Ⓝ 아미 ARMY   Ⓝ 우리 we, us   Ⓝ 선생님 teacher   Ⓝ 누구 who   Ⓝ 의사 doctor

N 에서 왔어요

N noun

✛ EASY to Use!

You can use this expression to say which country or region you are from.

country, region, etc. 에서 왔어요 → (저는) 미국 에서 왔어요.
I am from the United States.

✛ EASY to Speak!

- 이 사람은 브라질에서 왔어요.
  This person is from Brazil.

- 제 친구는 서울에서 왔어요.
  My friend is from Seoul.

- A : 어디에서 왔어요?
  Where are you from?
- B : 저는 태국에서 왔어요.
  I am from Thailand.

Tip!

You can also say what country or region you are from by using the expression "N¹은/는 N² 사람이에요" that you learned on page 26.

(저는) 프랑스에서 왔어요.
I am from France.
= (저는) 프랑스 사람이에요.
  I am French.

"N 에서 왔어요" is used when you are in a place that is not the country or region of your origin.

(When a Korean is in Korea)
저는 한국에서 왔어요. (×)
저는 한국 사람이에요. (✓)

Vocabulary
N 서울 Seoul N 어디 where

Where is BTS from? Complete the sentences.

저는 고양 사람이에요.

알엠은

고양에서 왔어요.

1

저는 과천 사람이에요.

진은

_____ .

2

저는 대구 사람이에요.

슈가는

_____ .

3

저는 광주 사람이에요.

제이홉은

_____ .

4

저는 부산 사람이에요.

지민은

_____ .

5

저는 대구 사람이에요.

뷔는

_____ .

6

저는 부산 사람이에요.

정국은

_____ .

Vocabulary

N 고양 Goyang   N 과천 Gwacheon   N 대구 Daegu   N 광주 Gwangju   N 부산 Busan

Dialogue

안녕하세요. 저는 케이트예요. 이름이 뭐예요?

 저는 슌이에요. 만나서 반가워요.

저도 만나서 반가워요. 저는 미국에서 왔어요.
슌 씨는 어디에서 왔어요?

 저는 일본 사람이에요.
어? 케이트 씨 방탄소년단 팬이에요?

네, 맞아요.

 와, 저도 아미예요. 우리 친하게 지내요.

Vocabulary

- 안녕하세요. Hello. • 만나서 반가워요. Nice to meet you. • 저도 me too N 씨 Mr./Ms. • 어? Oh!
- 네 yes • 맞아요. That's right. • 와 wow • 우리 친하게 지내요. Let's be friends.

30

1. Who did Kate meet? Where is he from?

2. What is your name? Where are you from?

3. Attach a photo of a friend or an artist you like, and fill in the table below. Then introduce them.

	Name	Country or Region	Job
	e.g. 진	한국	가수
	→ 이 사람은 진이에요. ...		

	Name	Country or Region	Job
	→		

Real Korean

Other ways to say "안녕하세요"

Are you familiar only with "안녕하세요"?
Try using different phrases to make your
conversation more natural when you first
meet someone.

- 안녕하세요.
  Hello.
- 안녕.
  Hi. (used with friends)
- (만나서) 반가워요.
  Nice to meet you.
- (앞으로) 잘 부탁드립니다.
  I hope to see you again.
  I look forward to working with you.
- 우리 친하게 지내요.
  Let's be friends.

"No, I'm not." Negative forms

We learned that "□¹은/는 □²이에요/예요" is
used to introduce something. To say
something is not something, you use the
expression "□¹은/는 □²이/가 아니에요."

- 저는 유학생이에요.
  I'm an international student.
  → 저는 유학생이 아니에요.
    I'm not an international student.
- 슌은 의사예요.
  Shun is a doctor.
  → 슌은 의사가 아니에요.
    Shun is not a doctor.

"안녕하세요. 방탄소년단입니다."

Have you ever been to a BTS concert? The feeling of seeing BTS perform in person is... indescribable. BTS' energy filling up the venue, fans cheering enthusiastically, ARMY BOMBs (the official BTS light stick) lighting up the darkness—all of this combines to create a truly magical time.

BTS 〈Yet To Come〉 in BUSAN

There is a greeting that BTS always uses at concerts. Let's shout it out together!

"둘, 셋! 방, 탄! 안녕하세요. 방탄소년단입니다."
"Two, three, BANGTAN! Hello. We are BTS."

You learned how to say "N 이에요/예요." "N 입니다" means the same thing, but is used in more formal settings. Until the day we hear the cheerful greetings of BTS again... Good luck with your Korean studies!

Create Your Own Vlog

Make a vlog introducing yourself in Korean.

"안녕하세요. 저는 ..."

내 방 투어

MY ROOM TOUR | KOREA VLOG

어서 오세요! 613

Welcome to My Room

 KATE

Learning Objective
#Introduce_Your_Space   #Say_the_Location   #Welcome_to_My_Room

33

Warm-up
Question

Imagine you invite BTS to your house-warming party.
What would you like to show them?

안녕하세요. 케이트예요!
Hi, I'm Kate!

짠! 여기는 제 방이에요. 제 방은 6층에 있어요.
Ta-da! This is my room. My room is on the 6th floor.

여기 책상이 있어요. 책상 위에 한국어 책이 있어요.
There is a desk here. There is a Korean textbook on the desk.

그리고 여기에 소파하고 옷장이 있어요.
And there is a sofa and a closet here.

핸드폰이... 어? 핸드폰이 없어요!
My cell phone is... Huh? My cell phone isn't here!

휴, 여기 있어요.
Phew, here it is.

그리고 저는 지금 침대 위에 있어요. 😃
And I'm on my bed right now.

 **Vocabulary**

 방 Room

✧ **What is in Kate's room? Check the vocabulary below.**

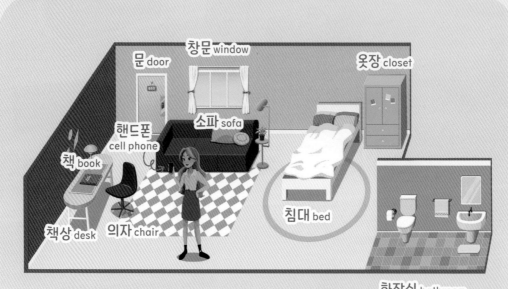

문 door
창문 window
옷장 closet
소파 sofa
핸드폰 cell phone
책 book
책상 desk
의자 chair
침대 bed
화장실 bathroom

Practice   What do you have in your room?

→ 제 방에는 _____ , _____ , _____ , _____ 이/가 있어요.

위치 Location

◇ Where is Kate? Use the vocabulary below to talk about specific locations.

위 above
집 house, home
안 inside
밖 outside
아래, 밑 under, below

뒤 back
오른쪽 right
왼쪽 left
앞 front
옆 side

Practice

1. Where is the cat?

→ 집 위 / 아래 에 있어요.

2. Are you inside or outside your room right now?

→ 저는 방 안 / 밖 에 있어요.

한자어 숫자 Chinese Character Numbers

◇ What floor is Kate's room on? Use the numbers below to say the number of floors, class periods, phone numbers, etc.

0	1	2	3	4	5	6	7
영*	일	이	삼	사	오	육	칠
8	9	10	11	12	20	30	...
팔	구	십	십일	십이	이십	삼십	

Floor	Class Period
●층	●교시
Phone Number	
●●●-●●●●-●●●●	

* When referring to a phone number, you read it as "공."

Practice Answer the following questions in Korean.

1. What floor is your room on?

2. What is your cell phone number?

Expression 1

N 이/가 있어요[없어요]

N noun
A adjective

⬦ EASY to Use!

If someone or something exists, or if someone possesses something, use "N 이/가 있어요." If not, use "N 이/가 없어요."

last syllable with batchim (e.g. 핸드폰)	이 있어요[없어요]	→	핸드폰이 있어요.
			I have a cell phone.

last syllable without batchim (e.g. 의자)	가 있어요[없어요]	→	의자가 없어요.
			There is no chair.

⬦ EASY to Speak!

- 아미밤이 있어요.
  I have an ARMY BOMB.

- 한국 친구가 있어요.
  I have a Korean friend.

- A : 수업이 있어요?
  Do you have a class?

  B1 : 네, 있어요.
  Yes, I do.

  B2 : 아니요, 없어요.
  No, I don't.

Tip!

When using this expression in conversations, "이/가" is often omitted. You can also use this expression to ask if something is available at a store.

A : 교통카드(가) 있어요?
Do you have transportation cards?

B : 네, 여기 있어요.
Yes, here you go.

When you want to make plans with someone, you can use this phrase to ask about their schedule. (See page 66)

케이트 씨, 시간(이) 있어요?
Kate, do you have time?

케이트 씨, 약속(이) 있어요?
Kate, do you have plans?

Vocabulary

A 있다 to be; to have • A 없다 to not be; to not have • N 아미밤 ARMY BOMB • N 수업 class • 아니요 no

N 교통카드 transportation card • N 시간 time • N 약속 plans

38

Practice

⏯ More practice

1. Match each word with the correct expression and complete the sentences.

Example	책 •			Example	책이 있어요 .
①	친구 •	• 이 있어요	①		_____ .
②	침대 •		②		_____ .
③	노트북 •	• 가 있어요	③		_____ .
④	지갑 •		④		_____ .

2. What do you need in the following situations? Choose the right word from the given words to complete the sentences.

교통카드   카메라   우산   티켓

I am trying to catch a bus.

Example

교통카드가 있어요 .

I am entering a concert venue.

1

_____ .

It is raining.

2

_____ .

I am trying to take a picture with BTS.

3

_____ .

Vocabulary

N 노트북 laptop   N 지갑 wallet   N 카메라 camera   N 우산 umbrella   N 티켓 ticket

N 에 있어요[없어요]

N noun

✧ EASY to Use!

You can use "N 에 있어요" when someone or something is in a specific location, and "N 에 없어요" when it is not.

location, place, etc. 에 있어요[없어요] → 제 방은 에 있어요.
My room is on the 6th floor.

✧ EASY to Speak!

- 케이트는 침대 위에 있어요.
  Kate is on the bed.

- 핸드폰이 책상 아래에 있어요.
  The cell phone is under the desk.

- 모자가 옷장 안에 없어요.
  The hat is not in the closet.

- 슌은 집에 없어요.
  Shun is not at home.

- A : 고양이가 없어요. 어디에 있어요?
  The cat is not here. Where is it?

- B : 의자 밑에 있어요.
  It is under the chair.

Tip!

By placing "N 에" at the beginning of the sentence, you can put more emphasis on the location or place.

책상 위에 한국어 책이 있어요.
On the desk, there is a Korean textbook.

여기에 옷장이 있어요.
Here, there is a closet.

"N 은/는" and "N 이/가" can both come in front of "N 에 있어요[없어요]." But when answering a question, you usually use "N 은/는."

A: 여자 화장실이 어디에 있어요?
Where is the women's restroom?

B: 여자 화장실은 3층에 있어요.
The women's restroom is on the 3rd floor.

Vocabulary

N 모자 hat N 고양이 cat N 한국어 Korean N 여자 woman (N 남자 man)

Find the objects in the room below and complete the sentences.

Q. 어디에 있어요?

아미밤

Example

한국어 책은 책상 위에 있어요.

① 케이트는 _____ .

② 고양이는 _____ .

③ 강아지는 _____ .

④ 아미밤은 _____ .

⑤ 방탄소년단 사진은 _____ .

Vocabulary

Ⓝ 강아지 puppy Ⓝ 사진 photo

Dialogue

 앗, 저 핸드폰이 없어요.

 정말요? 가방 안에 없어요?

 네, 없어요.

 케이트 씨, 핸드폰 번호가 뭐예요?

 010-0000-1234예요.

Shun calls Kate, and her cell phone rings

 어? 책상 아래에 있어요.

 와, 정말 고마워요.

 아니에요. 근데 케이트 씨, 한국어 책은 어디 있어요?

 아... 제 방에 있어요. 😊

Vocabulary

• 앗 oh no • 정말요? Really? N 가방 bag N 번호 number • 정말 really • 고마워요. Thank you.
• 아니에요. No problem. • 근데 but • 아 oh

42

Practice

1. Where was Kate's cell phone?　**1** 가방 안　　**2** 책상 아래　　**3** 케이트 방 안

2. Where do you usually put your belongings at home? Write the name of each item and its location.
   Then read them aloud.

Belongings	Q. 어디에 있어요?
e.g. 핸드폰	핸드폰은 침대 옆에 있어요.
핸드폰	
가방	
한국어 책	

 Real Korean

Asking more politely

You learned how to use "Ｎ이/가 뭐예요?" when asking for someone's name, job, or cell phone number, etc. You can also use "Ｎ이/가 어떻게 되세요?" to ask in a more polite way.

● 핸드폰 번호가 뭐예요?
  What's your cell phone number?
  → 핸드폰 번호가 어떻게 되세요?
    Could you tell me your cell phone number?

Express your feelings! Thanks and apologies

Here is how you say thank you and how to respond to it.

● A: 감사합니다. Thank you.
  B: 아니에요. No problem.

On the other hand, here is how to say sorry and how to respond to it.

● A: 죄송합니다. I'm sorry.
  B: 괜찮아요. It's okay.

For a more casual expression, you can also say "고마워요" ("Thanks") or "미안해요" ("Sorry").

집 구할 때 필요한 조건은? What Do You Look for in a Home?

호떡

You know 호세권 and 붕세권, right?

붕어빵

When you come to Korea, you will be looking for a place to stay. In any country, a place with convenient transportation nearby is very popular. In Seoul, the subway is very convenient, so homes near the station are very popular. In Korean, the area near the subway station is called 역세권 (area adjacent to a station). 역세권 is a combination of the words 역 (station) and 세권 (district).

But nowadays, in addition to 역세권, words like 호세권, and 붕세권 have emerged. In "[BANGTAN BOMB] Hotteok Time During Break," RM saw the *ho-tteok* that his staff bought and said, "You know 호세권 and 붕세권, right?" 호세권 and 붕세권 refer to the areas adjacent to street stalls that sell 호떡 (*ho-tteok*) and 붕어빵 (*bung-eo-ppang*), respectively. 호떡 is a snack that is made by pan-frying flour or glutinous rice flour dough stuffed with sugar filling. 붕어빵 is a fish shaped bun filled with sweet red bean paste or pastry cream.

호(호떡) + 세권 　│　 붕(붕어빵) + 세권

As these are popular Korean winter snacks, being able to buy 호떡 and 붕어빵 close to home is a huge plus. How about you? What do you look for in a home?

Create Your Own Vlog

Make a vlog introducing your place in Korean.

"여기는 제 방이에요. 제 방은 …"

Episode 3

내 가방 속에는?
#왓츠인마이백

TAKE A LOOK! WHAT'S IN MY BAG? | KOREA VLOG

What's in My Bag?

Easy Korean

 KATE

Learning Objective
#Describe_the_Items_in_Your_Bag   #My_Essentials

Warm-up
Question

♪Did you see my bag?♪
BTS' bag is probably full of trophies. 😎
What's in your bag? Do you have any BTS merch
that you always carry with you? Let us know!

안녕하세요. 케이트예요! 오늘은 '왓츠인마이백' 시간이에요.
Hi, I'm Kate! Today, it's time for a "What's in My Bag?"

이건 제 가방이에요. 물건이 아주 많아요.
This is my bag. I have a lot of things in it.

핸드폰이 있어요. 이건 제 텀블러예요. 조금 커요.
I have a cell phone. This is my tumbler. It's a bit big.

한국어 책이 두 권 있어요. 이 책 재미있어요. 어렵지 않아요.
I have two Korean textbooks. This book is interesting. It's not hard.

또... 핸드크림이 한 개 있어요. 향기가 정말 좋아요.
And... I have one tube of hand cream. It smells really good.

그리고 보조배터리가 있어요. 아, 이건 방탄소년단 사진이에요.
I also have a portable charger. Oh, this is a photo of BTS.

멤버들이 정말 멋져요. 😎
The members are really cool.

물건 Objects

⟡ What is in Kate's bag? You already learned some of the vocabulary words. Fill in the blanks.

가방 bag

(휴대용) 선풍기
(portable) fan

핸드크림
hand cream

2

이어폰
earphones

1

화장품
makeup

텀블러
tumbler

보조배터리
portable charger

고유어 숫자 Korean Numbers

⟡ You learned how to read some numbers on page 37. But there is one more set of numbers in Korean.
The following numbers are used to count things or to count the timing of something.

1	2	3	4	5	6	7
하나	둘	셋	넷	다섯	여섯	일곱
8	9	10	11	12	…	20
여덟	아홉	열	열하나	열둘	…	스물

⟡ When you count things, the number is followed by a unit. For example, you use "개" to count common
objects, "권" to count books, and "명" to count people.

한 개 or 하나	두 개	세 개	네 개	다섯 개	여섯 개	일곱 개
여덟 개	아홉 개	열 개	열한 개	열두 개	…	스무 개

"하나, 둘, 셋, 넷, 스물" become "한, 두, 세, 네, 스무" when you add a unit at the end.

Practice Count the number of objects or people.

1

핸드크림 _____

2

책 _____

3

사람 _____

형용사 Adjectives

✧ The tumbler in Kate's bag is big. Her hand cream smells good. The following words are used to describe the state of someone or something.

| 좋다 to be good | 나쁘다 to be bad | 많다 to be many | 적다 to be few | 예쁘다 to be pretty |

| 크다 to be big | 작다 to be small | 재미있다 to be funny | 재미없다 to be boring | 멋있다, 멋지다 to be cool |

| 편하다 to be comfortable | 불편하다 to be uncomfortable | 싸다 to be cheap | 비싸다 to be expensive |

Practice Find the opposite of the following words and write.

1 많다 ⟷ _____   2 좋다 ⟷ _____   3 작다 ⟷ _____

4 편하다 ⟷ _____   5 재미있다 ⟷ _____   6 비싸다 ⟷ _____

N 이/가 A 아/에/해요

N noun
A adjective

✛ EASY to Use!

You can use this expression with adjectives to describe the state of a person or thing. This expression is used in everyday speech in a polite manner.

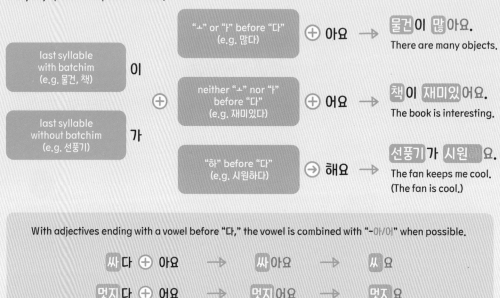

| last syllable with batchim (e.g. 물건, 책) | 이 |
| last syllable without batchim (e.g. 선풍기) | 가 |

⊕

"ㅗ" or "ㅏ" before "다" (e.g. 많다) ⊕ 아요 → 물건이 많아요. There are many objects.

neither "ㅗ" nor "ㅏ" before "다" (e.g. 재미있다) ⊕ 어요 → 책이 재미있어요. The book is interesting.

"하" before "다" (e.g. 시원하다) → 해요 → 선풍기가 시원해요. The fan keeps me cool. (The fan is cool.)

With adjectives ending with a vowel before "다," the vowel is combined with "-아/어" when possible.

싸다 ⊕ 아요 → 싸아요 → 싸요

멋지다 ⊕ 어요 → 멋지어요 → 멋져요

✛ EASY to Speak!

- 키가 조금 작아요.
  They are a little short.

- 라면이 맛있어요.
  The ramyeon is delicious.

- 소파가 아주 편해요.
  The sofa is very comfortable.

Tip!

When the syllable before "다" ends with the vowel "—," "—" is omitted. Then "-아/어요" is added depending on the vowel of the syllable before "—." If there is no syllable, "-어요" is added. (See page 167)

나쁘다 + 아요 → 나빠요

예쁘다 + 어요 → 예뻐요

크다 + 어요 → 커요

Vocabulary

A 시원하다 to be cool   **N** 키 height   • 조금 a little   • 키가 작다 to be short   **N** 라면 ramyeon
A 맛있다 to be delicious   • 아주 very

1. Complete the sentences by choosing the correct expressions.

❶ 기분 이 / 가 좋아요 / 좋어요 .

❷ 영화 이 / 가 재미없아요 / 재미없어요 .

❸ 직원 이 / 가 친절하요 / 친절해요 .

❹ 가방 이 / 가 크어요 / 커요 .

2. Answer the question using the given words.

Example

떡볶이, 맛있다

Q. 떡볶이가 어때요?
A. _____떡볶이가 맛있어요_____ .

1

한국어, 재미있다

Q. 한국어가 어때요?
A. _____ .

2

옷, 불편하다

Q. 옷이 어때요?
A. _____ .

3

패션, 멋지다

Q. 방탄소년난 패션이 어때요?
A. _____ .

Vocabulary

Ⓝ 기분 feeling　　Ⓝ 영화 movie　　Ⓝ 직원 staff　　Ⓐ 친절하다 to be friendly　　Ⓝ 떡볶이 *tteok-bo-kki*

• 어때요? How is it?　　Ⓝ 옷 clothes　　Ⓝ 패션 fashion

Ⓐ지 않다, 안 Ⓐ

Ⓐ adjective

✛ EASY to Use!

You can use this expression to negate the state of a person or thing. "Ⓐ지 않다" usually changes into "Ⓐ지 않아요" when it comes at the end of a sentence.

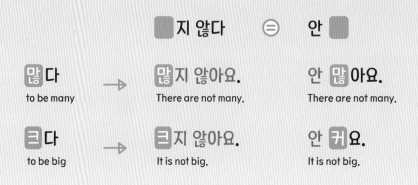

🟦지 않다 ＝ 안 🟦

많다
to be many

→

많지 않아요.
There are not many.

안 많아요.
There are not many.

크다
to be big

→

크지 않아요.
It is not big.

안 커요.
It is not big.

✛ EASY to Speak!

- 날씨가 좋지 않아요.
  The weather is not good.

- 가방이 안 예뻐요.
  The bag is not pretty.

- 화장품이 많지 않아요. 적어요.
  I don't have a lot of makeup. I have a little.

- A : 텀블러가 작아요?
  Is the tumbler small?

- B : 아니요, 안 작아요.
  No, it is not small.

> **Tip!**
>
> This expression is used in the negation of verbs as well as adjectives.

Ⓝ 날씨 weather

Answer the questions.

Example

Q. 머리가 짧아요?

A1. 아니요, 짧지 않아요.

A2. 아니요, 안 짧아요.

1

Q. 기분이 좋아요?

A1. 아니요, _____ .

A2. 아니요, _____ .

2

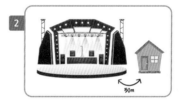

50m

Q. 콘서트장이 멀어요?

A1. 아니요, _____ .

A2. 아니요, _____ .

3

Q. 보조배터리가 커요?

A1. 아니요, _____ .

A2. 아니요, _____ .

4

Q. 사람이 적어요?

A1. 아니요, _____ .

A2. 아니요, _____ .

Vocabulary

N 머리 hair; head A 짧다 to be short N 콘서트 concert N 콘서트장 concert venue A 멀다 to be far

Dialogue

Kate takes out her portable fan

 케이트 씨, 그게 뭐예요?

아, 이건 '손선풍기'예요. 휴대용 선풍기예요.

 디자인이 정말 예뻐요. 그거 비싸요?

안 비싸요. 그리고 아주 시원해요.

Shun points to the photo on Kate's portable charger

 그건 방탄소년단 사진이에요?

네, 맞아요.

 역시 일곱 명 다 너무 멋있어요.

Vocabulary

N 손 hand N 손선풍기 handheld fan N 디자인 design • 그리고 and • 역시 as always • 다 all • 너무 very

Practice

1. Which words can describe Kate's portable fan? Check all of them.

☐ 안 비싸요   ☐ 불편해요   ☐ 예쁘지 않아요   ☐ 시원해요

2. Draw and describe your favorite object like the example below, and post it on social media.

이건 제 아미밤이에요. 정말 예뻐요. 크지 않아요.

Real Korean

Describe things more vividly!
Expressions of degree

When talking about something, you can describe it more vividly by adding expressions that show extent or degree.

- 아주 시원해요.
  It's very cool.
- 너무 멋있어요.
  It's so cool.
- 조금 커요.
  It's a bit big.
- 별로 안 비싸요.
  It's not that expensive.

- 진짜 좋아요.
  It's really good.
- 정말 예뻐요.
  It's really pretty.

※ "별로" is only used in negative sentences.

What is "이건"? Using abbreviations

Do you remember "이거," "그거," and "저거"? (See page 25) In real-life conversations, when these words are followed by "은/는" or "이/가," they are often shortened like this.

	은/는	이/가
이거 this	이건	이게
그거 that	그건	그게
저거 that	저건	저게

- A: 그게 뭐예요?
  What is that?
- B: 이건 '손선풍기'예요.
  This is a "handheld fan."

왓츠인마이콘서트백? 콘서트 가방 필수품 소개
What's in My Concert Bag? Concert Bag Essentials

What do you need to make your BTS concert experience 613%* perfect? Tickets, IDs, and ARMY BOMBs (the official BTS light stick) are just the basics! Here are some recommended items that are great to bring to a concert.

*June 13: BTS' debut date

BTS PERMISSION TO DANCE ON STAGE SEOUL

물
Water

You can get thirsty during the concert. You want to be careful though, as drinking too much water can lead to frequent visits to the restroom.

초콜릿
Chocolate

Chocolate is needed for replenishing energy every now and then. You can share it with your ARMY neighbors and talk about your ARMY journey.

망원경
Binoculars

Binoculars are recommended if your seat is far from the stage.

건전지
Batteries

It would be very sad if your ARMY BOMB's light went out in the middle of the concert.

보조배터리
Portable charger

It will allow you to charge your phone at the concert venue.

방석
Thin cushion

Place it on your seat so that sitting for a long time will not be a problem.

휴지심
Toilet paper tube

This is a great place to safely store the flyers handed out at concerts.

We also recommend talking to ARMY sitting next to you at the concert venue. "콘서트가 재미있어요!" "방탄소년단이 멋있어요!" Now let's enjoy the concert. Make some noise!

Create Your Own Vlog

Make a "What's in My Bag?" vlog to showcase your bag in Korean.

"제 가방이에요. 이건 …"

Episode 4

한국에서의 하루 일과

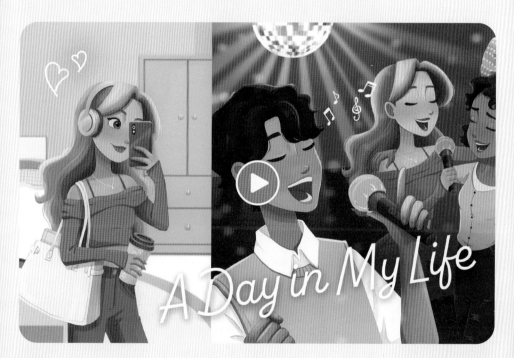

A DAY IN MY LIFE IN KOREA | KOREA VLOG

A Day in My Life

 KATE

Learning Objective

#Describe_a_Typical_Day   #Noraebang   #So_Much_Fun

Warm-up
Question

When do you listen to BTS songs and watch BTS videos? Tell us about your life as a BTS fan.

안녕하세요. 케이트예요! 오늘은 제 하루를 소개해요.
Hi, I'm Kate! Today I'll tell you about my day.

아침 8시 20분에 일어나요. 밥을 먹어요.
I wake up at 8:20 a.m. I eat breakfast.

오전 10시에 한국어 수업을 들어요. 배고파요! 12시에 점심을 먹어요.
I take a Korean class at 10:00 a.m. I'm hungry! I have lunch at 12:00 p.m.

저녁에 친구를 만나요. 같이 노래방에 가요.
I meet my friend in the evening. We go to a *noraebang* together.

우리는 방탄소년단 노래를 좋아해요.
We like BTS songs.

저녁 8시 반에 집에 와요. 그리고 방탄소년단 영상을 봐요.
I come home at 8:30 p.m. And I watch BTS videos.

벌써 11시예요. 잘 자요! 😴
It's already 11:00 p.m. Good night!

시간 Time

✛ Kate introduced her day while mentioning the time. This is how we say the time in Korean.

☀   오전 a.m.   12:00 p.m.   오후 p.m.   ☽

아침	점심	낮	저녁	밤
morning, breakfast	afternoon, lunch	daytime	evening, dinner	night

"아침, 점심, 저녁" can also refer to meals as well as times of day!

✛ You can use "시" and "분" to refer to specific times. When you want to ask the time, you can say "몇 시예요?" ("What time is it?")

Korean numbers ⊕ 시	Chinese character numbers ⊕ 분
(한, 두, 세, … → See page 48)	(일, 이, 삼, … → See page 37)

한 시	01	:	01	일 분
두 시	02	:	02	이 분
세 시	03	:	05	오 분
네 시	04	:	30	삼십 분
열한 시	11	:	55	오십오 분
열두 시	12	:	59	오십구 분

AM 06:13
오전 여섯 시 십삼 분

PM 11:00
오후 열한 시

Instead of "오전, 오후," you can say "아침, 낮, 저녁, 밤."

PM 08:30
여덟 시 삼십 분
여덟 시 반

"반" means "half."

동사 Verbs

Let's take a look at Kate's day again. The vocabulary below is used to describe actions.

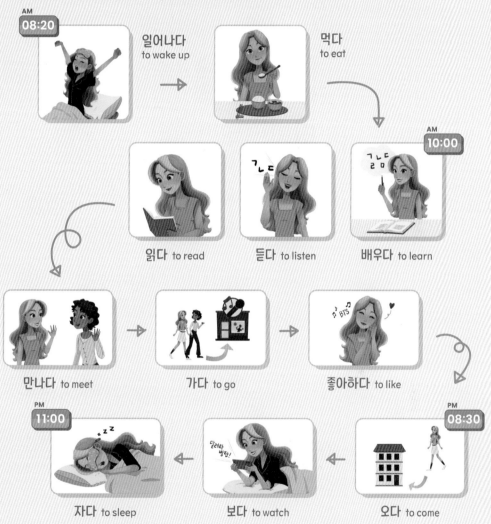

AM 08:20

일어나다 to wake up

먹다 to eat

읽다 to read

듣다 to listen

AM 10:00

배우다 to learn

만나다 to meet

가다 to go

좋아하다 to like

PM 08:30

오다 to come

보다 to watch

PM 11:00

자다 to sleep

 Practice Answer the following questions in Korean.

1. What time does Kate have her Korean classes?

2. What time does Kate get home?

3. What time does Kate go to bed?

4. What time do you usually go to bed?

N 을/를 V 아/어/해요

N noun
V verb

⬦ EASY to Use!

You can use this expression with verbs to describe an action in polite, everyday speech.
"N을/를" is used to refer to the object of action, but "을/를" is often omitted in real-life conversations.

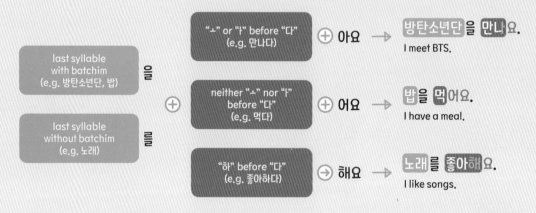

last syllable
with batchim
(e.g. 방탄소년단, 밥)

을

last syllable
without batchim
(e.g. 노래)

를

⊕

"ㅗ" or "ㅏ" before "다"
(e.g. 만나다) ⊕ 아요 → 방탄소년단을 만나요.
I meet BTS.

neither "ㅗ" nor "ㅏ"
before "다"
(e.g. 먹다) ⊕ 어요 → 밥을 먹어요.
I have a meal.

"하" before "다"
(e.g. 좋아하다) → 해요 → 노래를 좋아해요.
I like songs.

With verbs ending with a vowel before "다,"
the vowel is combined with "-아/어" when possible.

사다 ⊕ 아요 → 사아요 → 사요

보다 ⊕ 아요 → 보아요 → 봐요

배우다 ⊕ 어요 → 배우어요 → 배워요

마시다 ⊕ 어요 → 마시어요 → 마셔요

되다 ⊕ 어요 → 되어요 → 돼요

빼다 ⊕ 어요 → 빼어요 → 빼요

Tip!

Use "에" instead of "을/를" after a place name when using the verbs "가다" (to go) and "오다" (to come) to indicate the destination of movement.

A: 어디에 가요?
   Where are you going?
B: 학교에 가요.
   I am going to school.

The batchim "ㄷ" in "듣다" (to listen) and "걷다" (to walk) changes to "ㄹ" when they are combined with an expression that begins with a vowel. (See page 167)

듣다 + 어요 → 들어요

걷다 + 어요 → 걸어요

Vocabulary

V 하다 to do   N 밥 meal; rice   N 노래 song   V 사다 to buy   V 마시다 to drink   V 되다 to become; to be okay

V 빼다 to remove, to leave out   N 학교 school   V 걷다 to walk

What is BTS doing? Answer the questions using the given words.

Q. 진이 뭐 해요?

A. ___게임을 해요___ . (게임, 하다)

Q. 알엠하고 뷔가 뭐 해요?

A. _____ . (전화, 하다)

Q. 슈가가 뭐 해요?

A. _____ . (책, 읽다)

Q. 제이홉이 뭐 해요?

A. _____ . (TV, 보다)

Q. 지민이 뭐 해요?

A. _____ . (치킨, 먹다)

Q. 정국이 뭐 해요?

A. _____ . (음료수, 마시다)

Vocabulary

• 뭐 해요? What are you doing?   N 게임 game   • 하고 and   N 전화 phone   N 치킨 fried chicken
N 음료수 beverage

에

Ⓝ noun

✛ EASY to Use!

You can use this expression to say the time.

아침 에 샤워를 해요.
I take a shower in the morning.

time 에 → 열두 시 에 점심을 먹어요.
I eat lunch at 12:00.

밤 열한 시 에 자요.
I sleep at 11:00 at night.

✛ EASY to Speak!

- 오전에 수업을 들어요.
  I take a class in the morning.

- 저녁 여덟 시 반에 집에 와요.
  I get home at 8:30 in the evening.

- A : 오늘 몇 시에 친구를 만나요?
  (오늘 언제 친구를 만나요?)
  What time are you meeting your friend today?
  (When are you meeting your friend today?)

- B : 오후 두 시에 만나요.
  I am meeting my friend at 2:00 p.m.

| **Tip!** |

"에" is not used after "지금" (now), "오늘" (today), "어제" (yesterday) and "내일" (tomorrow).

지금 뭐 해요?
What are you doing now?

저는 오늘 친구하고 운동을 해요.
I will do a workout with my friend today.

Vocabulary

Ⓝ 샤워 shower • 오늘 today Ⓝ 몇 시 what time • 언제 when • 지금 now • 어제 yesterday • 내일 tomorrow
Ⓝ 운동 workout

Practice

The following is Kate's daily schedule. Write the time and complete the sentences.

Daily Schedule

오전	8:20	**Example** 오전 여덟 시 이십 분에 일어나요.
	10:00	① _____ 한국어 수업을 들어요.
		점심
		춤 연습 (dance practice)
오후	6:13	② _____ 친구를 만나요. 같이 노래방에 가요.
	10:15	③ _____ 방탄소년단 영상을 봐요.
	11:00	④ _____ 자요.

 V o c a b u l a r y

• 같이 together Ⓝ 노래방 *noraebang* Ⓝ 영상 video

 숲 씨, 보통 저녁에 뭐 해요?

 컴퓨터 게임 해요. 케이트 씨는 저녁에 뭐 해요?

 저는 친구들하고 같이 놀아요. 오늘은 노래방에 가요.

 와, 노래방!

 숲 씨, 노래 좋아해요?

 네, 좋아해요. 방탄소년단 노래를 특히 좋아해요.

 대박! 오늘 저녁 7시에 시간 있어요? 우리 같이 놀아요.

 좋아요!

Vocabulary

• 보통 usually Ⓝ 컴퓨터 computer • -들 -s (plural) Ⓥ 놀다 to hang out • 특히 especially • 대박! Awesome!

66

1. What is Shun doing tonight?

2. Do you have a daily routine? Write down your own routine and talk about it in Korean.

Time	Activity	Your Routine
e.g. 오전 여덟 시	일어나다	오전 여덟 시에 일어나요.

Real Korean

♪Still with you ♪ "하고"

"하고" has two meanings. First, it has the meaning of "and" and is used to list objects.

- 핸드폰하고 보조배터리가 있어요.
  There is a cell phone and a portable charger.
- 떡볶이하고 치킨을 좋아해요.
  I like *tteok-bo-kki* and fried chicken.

It can also refer to someone who you are doing something with.

- 친구하고 저녁을 먹어요.
  I'm having dinner with a friend.

"같이 해요!" Make a suggestion

"아/어/해요" can also be used with "같이" to suggest doing something together.

- A: 우리 같이 노래방에 가요!
  Let's go to the *noraebang* together!
- B: 좋아요.
  Okay, great.

방탄소년단처럼 코인 노래방 즐기기
Enjoy Coin *Noraebang* Like BTS

If you are a fan of BTS, there is a must-visit place in Korea. It is full of upbeat music and colorful lights... It's the 코인 노래방 (coin *noraebang*)! 코인 노래방 is a place with many small booth-type 노래방 (*noraebang*) where you can sing songs to your heart's content with instrumental accompaniment. Korean *noraebang* features instrumental accompaniment for many BTS hits.

BTS (방탄소년단) 'Butter' in 노래방

In the video "[2020 FESTA] BTS (방탄소년단) 'MAP OF THE SONG : 7'," BTS had fun at a coin *noraebang*. They were on a mission to sing each other's songs. Jimin, V, and Jung Kook sang the rappers' song "욱 (UGH!)," RM and Jin sang Jung Kook's "Euphoria," and SUGA and j-hope sang the vocalists' song, "The Truth Untold (Feat. Steve Aoki)." Everyone brought their own charm into their performance.

If you want to sing BTS songs at the top of your lungs, why not try visiting a coin *noraebang*? Not only will your singing skills improve, but your Korean will improve as well. You can kill two birds with one stone!

Create Your Own Vlog

Make a vlog describing your day in Korean.

"오늘 제 하루를 소개해요. 저는 ..."

Episode 5 한국 음식 먹방

KOREAN FOOD MUKBANG | KOREA VLOG

꿀잼시작 Mukbang!

KATE

Learning Objective
#Order_Food   #Pay_the_Bill   #Yummy

Warm-up
Question

There are many videos featuring BTS eating Korean foods. Have you ever tried Korean foods? Out of all the Korean foods BTS ate, which would you like to try the most?

안녕하세요. 케이트예요! 오늘 광장시장에 처음 가요.
Hi, I'm Kate! Today, I'm going to Gwangjang Market for the first time.

너무 기대돼요!
I'm so excited!

광장시장은 길거리 음식이 정말 많아요.
Gwangjang Market has a lot of street food.

김밥, 빈대떡, 육회, 떡볶이가 유명해요.
Gimbap, mung bean pancake, beef tartare, and *tteok-bo-kki* are famous.

뭐 먹을까요? 김밥을 먹을까요, 떡볶이를 먹을까요? 😊
What should we eat? Should we have *gimbap* or *tteok-bo-kki*?

어우, 너무 배고파요. 와, 저 식당 보세요. 사람이 진짜 많아요.
Oh, I'm so hungry. Wow, look at that restaurant. There are so many people.

혹시 맛집? 우리 저기 갈까요? 고고!
Is it a popular restaurant? Should we go there? Let's go!

가격 Prices

✧ Kate goes to a popular restaurant in Gwangjang Market. Before you go to a restaurant, you will want to make sure you have Korean money. Korea uses "원" (won) as its unit of currency. Amounts of Korean money are expressed using Chinese character numbers (일, 이, 삼, … → see page 37), and large numbers like the ones below are often used, so keep them in mind!

100	200	300	…	1,000	1,100	1,200	…
백	이백	삼백	…	천	천백	천이백	…

2,000	3,000	…	10,000	100,000	1,000,000
이천	삼천	…	만	십만	백만

✧ Korean money looks like this:

백 원
오백 원
천 원
오천 원
만 원
오만 원

Practice   Look at the menu on page 73. Write the prices in Korean.

Example 라면은 얼마예요? How much is the *ramyeon*?   _삼천구백_   원이에요.

❶ 떡볶이는 얼마예요? How much is the *tteok-bo-kki*?   _____   원이에요.

❷ 삼겹살은 얼마예요? How much is the *sam-gyeop-sal*?   _____   원이에요.

음식 Foods

✛ What do you think Kate will order at the popular restaurant in Gwangjang Market? Let's look at the menu together.

MENU 메뉴

Rice

김밥
gimbap
₩3,500

비빔밥
bibimbap
₩8,500

김치볶음밥
kimchi bo-kkeum-bap
₩7,800

Bunsik (simple flour-based foods)

떡볶이
tteok-bo-kki
1인분 ₩4,500

순대
sun-dae
1인분 ₩5,000

빈대떡
mung bean pancake
₩5,000

야채튀김
deep-fried vegetables
₩2,000

Noodles

라면
ramyeon
₩3,900

냉면
naeng-myeon
₩9,500

짜장면
jja-jang-myeon
₩6,500

Meat

삼겹살
sam-gyeop-sal
1인분(200g) ₩15,000

치킨
fried chicken
1마리 ₩19,000

육회
beef tartare
₩20,000

밥, 공깃밥
rice,
a bowl of rice

김치
kimchi

Practice Answer the following questions in Korean.

1. What are some of the noodle dishes?

2. What are some of the *bunsik* foods?

Tip!

Different foods have different units.

Foods	Units	Numbers
common foods	개	한 개, 두 개, 세 개, …
	인분 (serving)	일 인분, 이 인분, 삼 인분, …
김밥	줄 (roll)	한 줄, 두 줄, 세 줄, …
치킨	마리 (animal)	한 마리, 두 마리, 세 마리, …

Expression 1

V (으)ㄹ까요?

V verb

✧ EASY to Use!

You can use this expression to ask for someone's opinion about an action. It is often used to suggest doing something together, in which case it is often used with "같이" (together).

| with batchim before "다" (excluding "ㄹ") (e.g. 먹다) | ⊕ 을까요? → | 뭐 먹을까요?
What should we eat? |

| without batchim or with batchim "ㄹ" before "다" ("ㄹ" is dropped) (e.g. 주문하다, 만들다) | ⊕ ㄹ까요? | 김밥을 주문할까요?
Should we order *gimbap*? |
| | | 같이 김치볶음밥을 만들까요?
Should we make *kimchi bo-kkeum-bap* together? |

✧ EASY to Speak!

- 사진을 찍을까요?
  Should we take a picture?

- 같이 영화를 볼까요?
  Should we watch a movie together?

- 방탄소년단 노래를 들을까요?   듣다 Irregular Conjugation (p. 167)
  Should we listen to a BTS song?

- A : 내일 같이 놀까요?
  Should we hang out together tomorrow?

  B : 좋아요. 같이 놀아요.
  Yes. Let's hang out.

Tip!

To agree to someone's request to do something together, you can reply with "좋아요" or "그래요." To decline, instead of just saying "아니요" (no), it is better to apologize and explain your reason for declining.

A : 점심 같이 먹을까요?
Should we have lunch together?

B : 미안해요. 다른 약속이 있어요.
Sorry. I have other plans.

다음에 같이 먹어요.
Let's have lunch next time.

Vocabulary

🅥 주문하다 to order 🅥 만들다 to make 🅥 찍다 to take (a picture) • 그래요. Okay. • 미안해요. Sorry.
• 다른 other   • 다음에 next time

Choose the right words from the given words and ask BTS to do the activities with you.

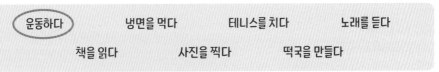

| 운동하다 | 냉면을 먹다 | 테니스를 치다 | 노래를 듣다 |
| 책을 읽다 | 사진을 찍다 | 떡국을 만들다 | |

Example

정국 씨, 같이 **운동할까요**?

1 뷔 씨, 같이 _____?

2 지민 씨, 같이 _____?

3 제이홉 씨, 같이 _____?

4 슈가 씨, 같이 _____?

5 진 씨, 같이 _____?

6 알엠 씨, 같이 _____?

Vocabulary

Ⓥ 운동하다 to work out   Ⓝ 테니스 tennis   Ⓥ 치다 to hit; to play   • 테니스를 치다 to play tennis
Ⓝ 떡국 *tteok-guk* (sliced rice cake soup)

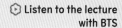

 Ⅴ (으)세요

Ⅴ verb

✧ EASY to Use!

You can use this expression to politely instruct the listener to do something. It is usually used when ordering food in which case you can say "주세요."

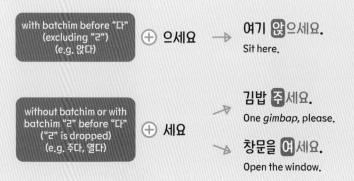

| with batchim before "다" (excluding "ㄹ") (e.g. 앉다) | ⊕ 으세요 | → | 여기 **앉**으세요. Sit here. |

| without batchim or with batchim "ㄹ" before "다" ("ㄹ" is dropped) (e.g. 주다, 열다) | ⊕ 세요 | ↗ 김밥 **주**세요. One *gimbap*, please. ↘ 창문을 **여**세요. Open the window. |

✧ EASY to Speak!

- 전화를 받으세요.
  Pick up the phone.

- 빨리 오세요.
  Come quickly.

- 수업을 들으세요. [듣다 Irregular Conjugation (p. 167)]
  Take a class.

- A : 뭐 드릴까요?
  What can I get for you?

- B : 라면 하나 주세요.
  One *ramyeon*, please.

Tip!

When you combine "먹다" (to eat) with "-(으)세요," it becomes "드세요."

맛있게 드세요.
Enjoy your meal.

ᴠᴏᴄᴀʙᴜʟᴀʀʏ

Ⅴ 앉다 to sit　Ⅴ 주다 to give　Ⓝ 창문 window　Ⅴ 열다 to open　Ⅴ 받다 to pick up; to receive　• 빨리 quickly

Ⅴ 드리다 to give (honorific)　• 맛있게 드세요. Enjoy your meal.

1. Complete the sentences using the given words and "**V**(으)세요."

Example

가다

병원에 가세요 .

1
일어나다

일찍 _____ .

2
읽다

메시지를 _____ .

3
잡다

어깨를 _____ .

2. You are at a restaurant. Order the correct amount of food.

Example
냉면, 개 → 냉면 두 개 주세요 .

1
김밥, 줄 → _____ .

2
치킨, 마리 → _____ .

3
1인분
삼겹살, 인분 → _____ .

우리 뭐 먹을까요?

 김밥 두 줄하고 떡볶이 어때요?

좋아요. 빈대떡도 시킬까요?

 그래요. (calls to the waiter) 여기요!

 네, 뭐 드릴까요?

 김밥 두 줄, 떡볶이 하나, 빈대떡 하나 주세요.

after the meal

잘 먹었습니다. 얼마예요?

 만 육천오백 원입니다.

〰 Vocabulary

- ... 어때요? How about...?   • 도 also   **V** 시키다 to order   • 여기요. Excuse me.
- 잘 먹었습니다. Thanks for the great food.   • 얼마예요? How much is it?

Practice

1. What did Kate and Shun order? How much was everything?

2. Look at the menu on page 73 again and order the food you want to eat. How many dishes will you order? How much is it in total?

김치볶음밥 하나, 짜장면 하나 주세요.
만 사천삼백 원이에요.

Real Korean

Dine out like a local at a Korean restaurant!

Are you worried about not being able to understand the staff at a Korean restaurant? If you know the phrases below, you will not have to worry!

- 어서 오세요.
  Welcome.

- 몇 분이세요?
  Table for how many?

- 이쪽으로 오세요.
  Come this way.

- 편하신 데 앉으세요.
  Take a seat wherever you'd like.

- 주문하시겠어요?
  Would you like to order?

- 뭐 드릴까요?
  What can I get for you?

Knowing how to say these phrases will also be useful.

- 주문할게요.
  I'd like to order, please.

- 계산할게요.
  Bill, please.

I like it, too! "□도"

When you want to add something else to someone or something you already mentioned, you add "도" after the noun. "도" goes in place of "은/는" or "을/를."

- 라면을 먹어. 떡볶이도 먹어.
  I eat *ramyeon*. I also eat *tteok-bo-kki*.

- A: 저는 방탄소년단을 좋아해요.
  I like BTS.
  B: 저도 방탄소년단을 좋아해요.
  I also like BTS.

방탄소년단이 만장일치로 주문한 '짜파구리'
BTS' Unanimous Order of *Jja-pa-gu-ri*

Have you heard of 먹방? 먹방 is short for 먹는 방송 (eating broadcast), which is a broadcast that introduces food and shows people eating it. When it comes to 먹방, you cannot leave out BTS!

In 〈Run BTS!〉 EP. 150-151 "War of Money Hotel Staycation," everyone in BTS ordered 짜파구리 and showed us a 먹방. 짜파구리, also known as "Ram-don," is a type of *jja-jang bi-bim-myeon* dish made by mixing *jja-jang ramyeon* and regular *ramyeon*. It is an appealing noodle dish that combines the richness of *jja-jang ramyeon* with the spiciness of regular *ramyeon*. 짜파구리 became a popular dish in Korea due to the internet and later became known worldwide after it was featured in the movie 〈Parasite (2019)〉.

In addition to 먹방, there is also the term 쿡방, which means cooking broadcast. It is a combination of 쿡, the Korean pronunciation of "cook," and 방송 (broadcast). BTS is known for their 쿡방 as well. In 〈IN THE SOOP BTS ver.〉 and 〈BTS BON VOYAGE〉, they cooked and ate dishes such as 김치찌개 (*kimchi jji-gae*), 닭갈비 (*dak-gal-bi*), and 칼국수 (*kal-guk-su*).

If you want to learn more about recipes made by BTS, check out the 〈BTS RECIPE BOOK〉 series!

What are some famous Food Alleys in your neighborhood?
Make a vlog exploring the alleys and finding popular restaurants.

"오늘 0000에 가요. 뭐 먹을까요? ..."

 **Episode 6**

같이 공부해요!
#스터디윗미

LET'S STUDY TOGETHER! STUDY WITH ME | KOREA VLOG

 KATE

Learning Objective

#Talk_About_Past_Activities   #Talk_About_Your_Studies   #Study_Hard

Warm-up
Question

Do you listen to songs when you study or work on
something that requires concentration? If so,
are they BTS songs? Let us know the playlist you listen to!

안녕하세요. 케이트예요! 내일 시험이 있어요.
Hi, I'm Kate! I have a test tomorrow.

오늘은 저하고 같이 공부해요! 열공!
Study with me today! Let's study hard!

(a few hours later)
와, 벌써 9시 반이에요. 이제 집에 갈까요?
Wow, it's already 9:30. Why don't we go home now?

(on the way home)
저 스터디 카페에서 정말 열심히 공부했어요. 한국어 단어를 다 외웠어요.
I studied so hard at the study café. I memorized all the Korean words.

대화를 10번 정도 읽었어요. 문제도 진짜 많이 풀었어요.
I read the dialogues about 10 times. I solved a lot of problems.

그리고 이건 비밀! 〈달려라 방탄〉도 조금 봤어요. 😄
And don't tell anyone! But I watched a little bit of 〈Run BTS!〉 as well.

Vocabulary

장소 Places

↪ There are many different places in Kate's neighborhood.

병원 hospital

식당 restaurant

약국 pharmacy

백화점 department store
쇼핑몰 shopping mall

카페 café

코인 노래방 coin *noraebang*

스터디 카페 study café

회사 company, office

공원 park

영화관 movie theater

편의점 convenience store

Practice Where did Kate study today? (See page 83)

→ _____ 에서 공부했어요.

학습 Study

✧ Kate studied really hard today. Let's take a look at words and expressions related to studying.

공부하다 to study

단어 word

말하다 to speak　　**쓰다** to write　　**외우다** to memorize　　**쉬다** to rest

알다 to know

모르다 to not know

문제를 풀다 to solve problems

펜 pen

시험 test

노트북 laptop

공책 notebook

Practice　What methods is Kate using to study?
From the following, choose the method that Kate is not using on this page.

❶ 문제를 풀어요.　　❷ 한국어를 말해요.　　❸ 단어를 외워요.　　❹ 한국어를 들어요.

에서

N noun

✧ EASY to Use!

You can use this expression to talk about the location of a particular action.

카페 에서 친구를 만나요.
I meet a friend at a café.

place 에서 → 집 에서 청소해요.
I clean at home.

백화점 에서 쇼핑해요.
I shop at a department store.

✧ EASY to Speak!

- 공원에서 운동해요.
  I work out in the park.

- 편의점에서 물을 사요.
  I buy water at a convenience store.

- A : 어디에서 공부해요?
  Where do you study?
- B : 스터디 카페에서 공부해요.
  I study at a study café.

Tip!

When using "있다" (to be; to have)/
"없다" (to not be; to not have) (p. 40) and
"가다" (to go)/"오다" (to come) (p. 62),
you need to add "에" after the noun
indicating the place.

화장실이 1층에 있어요.
The restroom is on the 1st floor.

케이트 씨가 학교에 가요.
Kate goes to school.

v o c a b u l a r y

V 청소하다 to clean **V** 쇼핑하다 to shop **N** 물 water

1. What are Kate and Shun doing at the following locations? Complete the sentences.

Example

케이트가 공원에 가요.
<u>공원에서</u> 산책해요.

1

케이트가 약국에 가요.
_____ 약을 사요.

2

숨이 집에 있어요.
_____ 자요.

3

케이트하고 숨이 카페에 있어요.
_____ 커피를 마셔요.

2. Answer the questions using the given words.

1

Q. 어디에서 영화를 봐요?

영화관

A. _____ .

2

Q. 어디에서 일해요?

회사

A. _____ .

3

Q. 방탄소년단이
어디에서 밥을 먹어요?

식당

A. _____ .

4

Q. 여러분은
어디에서 공부해요?

?

your own answer

A. _____ .

ⓥ⍥ⓒⓐⓑⓤⓛⓐⓡⓨ

Ⓥ 산책하다 to take a walk Ⓝ 약 medicine Ⓝ 커피 coffee Ⓥ 일하다 to work Ⓝ 여러분 everyone

Episode 6. Let's Study Together! Study with Me **87**

A/V 았/었/했어요

A/V adjective or verb

✧ EASY to Use!

You can use this expression to talk about something that happened in the past or something that has been completed.

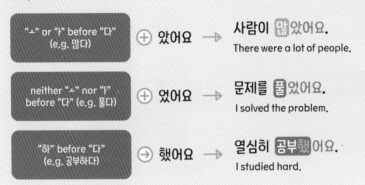

"ㅗ" or "ㅏ" before "다" (e.g. 많다)	⊕ 았어요 →	사람이 많았어요. There were a lot of people.
neither "ㅗ" nor "ㅏ" before "다" (e.g. 풀다)	⊕ 었어요 →	문제를 풀었어요. I solved the problem.
"하" before "다" (e.g. 공부하다)	⊖ 했어요 →	열심히 공부했어요. I studied hard.

With adjectives or verbs ending with a vowel before "다," the vowel is combined with "-았/었-" when possible. (See page 62)

✧ EASY to Speak!

- 집에 일찍 돌아왔어요.
  I came back home early.

- 식당에서 점심을 먹었어요.
  I had lunch at a restaurant.

- 방이 깨끗했어요.
  The room was clean.

- 어제 정말 바빴어요. ⟵ "ㅡ" Elimination (p. 167)
  I was really busy yesterday.

- A : 어제 뭐 했어요?
  What did you do yesterday?

- B : 집에서 쉬었어요.
  I rested at home.

Tip!

When "-아/어/해" or "-았/었/했-" comes after verbs or adjectives with "르" before "다," like "모르다" (to not know), the "르" usually changes to "ㄹㄹ." (See page 167)

모르다 + 았어요	부르다 + 었어요
↓	↓
모ㄹㄹ + 았어요	부ㄹㄹ + 었어요
↓	↓
몰랐어요	불렀어요

이름을 몰랐어요.
I did not know the name.

노래를 불렀어요.
I sang the song.

Vocabulary

• 열심히 hard **V** 돌아오다 to come back **A** 깨끗하다 to be clean **A** 바쁘다 to be busy **V** 부르다 to sing; to call

1. What did BTS do in 〈Run BTS!〉? Complete the sentences by choosing the correct expressions.

먹다

① 라면을 먹았어요 / 먹었어요 .

요리하다

② 요리핬어요 / 요리했어요 .

만나다

③ 다른 멤버를 만났어요 / 만나었어요 .

부르다

④ 노래를 부렀어요 / 불렀어요 .

2. This is Shun's diary. Complete the sentences using the given words.

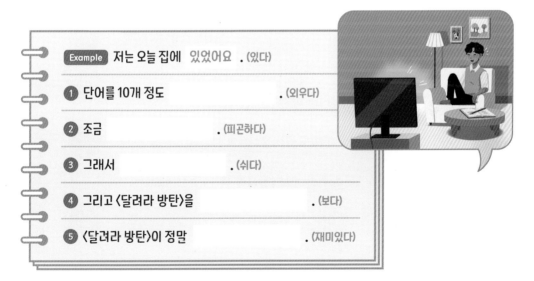

Example 저는 오늘 집에 있었어요 . (있다)

① 단어를 10개 정도   . (외우다)

② 조금   . (피곤하다)

③ 그래서   . (쉬다)

④ 그리고 〈달려라 방탄〉을   . (보다)

⑤ 〈달려라 방탄〉이 정말   . (재미있다)

Ⓥ Ⓞ Ⓒ Ⓐ Ⓑ Ⓤ Ⓛ Ⓐ Ⓡ Ⓨ

Ⓥ 요리하다 to cook   Ⓝ 멤버 member   Ⓝ 정도 degree; about   Ⓐ 피곤하다 to be tired   • 그래서 so

• 달려라 방탄 Run BTS! (BTS' original video series)

the morning of the test

 케이트 씨, 시험 공부 많이 했어요?

네. 어제 하루 종일 스터디 카페에서 공부만 했어요.
숀 씨도 많이 했어요?

 아니요, 저는 별로 안 했어요. 😂
어제 집에서 〈달려라 방탄〉만 봤어요.

숀 씨도 봤어요? 어제 정말 재미있었어요!

 어? 어제 스터디 카페에서 〈달려라 방탄〉도 봤어요?

에이, 조금 봤어요. 곧 시험 시작해요. 우리 모두 파이팅!

 네, 파이팅! 😁

Vocabulary

Ⓝ 공부 study　　• 많이 a lot　• 하루 종일 all day　• 만 only　• 별로 (not) that much

• 에이 well (aw, come on)　• 곧 soon　Ⓥ 시작하다 to start　• 모두 all　• 파이팅! Let's do this!

90

1. What did Kate do yesterday? Check all the correct answers.

☐ 공부했어요. ☐ 〈달려라 방탄〉을 봤어요. ☐ 집에서 쉬었어요. ☐ 시험을 봤어요.

2. What did you do yesterday? Write and talk about it. Post it on social media with some photos you took yesterday.

Example ⋯	Me ⋯
 어제 멤버들하고 떡볶이를 먹었어요. 순대도 먹었어요. 모두 너무 맛있었어요. 그리고 공연을 했어요. 정말 재미있었어요.	_____ _____ _____

Real Korean

Let's do this! 파이팅!

In Korea, when you want to cheer someone on, you can shout out "파이팅!" This comes from the English word "fighting," but it does not mean to fight. You can often see BTS shouting "파이팅" to each other when they are competing or playing games on 〈Run BTS!〉. Sometimes it is pronounced as "화이팅."

You can also cheer someone on with the following expressions.

- 힘내요.
  Hang in there.
- 아자 아자!
  Let's go!

Only you, "N만"

When you are talking about one thing in specific and excluding everything else, you add "만" to the noun. You can put it in the place of "이/가" or "을/를."

- 저만 왔어요. (다른 사람은 안 왔어요.)
  I'm the only one that came.
  (No one else came.)
- 케이크는 안 먹었어요. 커피만 마셨어요.
  I didn't eat any cake. I only drank coffee.

한국의 졸업식과 수능
Korean Graduation and the College Scholastic Ability Test

BTS (방탄소년단) MBTI Lab

What type of education curriculum do the children in your country or region go through as they become adults? In Korea, children usually go through six years of elementary school, three years of middle school, and high school, respectively.

As high school graduation marks the beginning of adulthood, people find it meaningful, just as BTS did. On Jung Kook's graduation day, all members participated and congratulated him. They also visited the Chinese restaurant they had gone to for his entrance ceremony and had a good time chatting with each other as they shared 쟁반짜장 (*jaeng-ban jja-jang*). During a live performance of the album ⟨Proof⟩, when talking about the best moment in his life, Jung Kook mentioned that this time came to mind.

The College Scholastic Ability Test (수능) is an important test for getting into university. In the past, BTS packed lunches for other members who were taking the CSAT to show their support.

The CSAT is a very important test in Korea, as shown by the large number of test takers. So it also involves some interesting customs. Test takers are often given gifts of 엿 (*yeot* or malt candy) and 찹쌀떡 (*chap-ssal-tteok* or sweet rice cake with red bean filling). Since the *yeot* and *chap-ssal-tteok* are sticky, it is meant to help them "stick to" or get accepted into the university of their choice. On the other hand, *mi-yeok-guk* (seaweed soup) is not eaten on the day of the test because it is superstitiously believed that the slippery texture of seaweed will cause test takers to "slip" on the test.

Create Your Own Vlog

Where did you go and what did you do yesterday?
Make a vlog that summarizes your day yesterday.

"저는 어제 OOO에서 OO했어요. ...."

Episode 7
한국 카페 투어

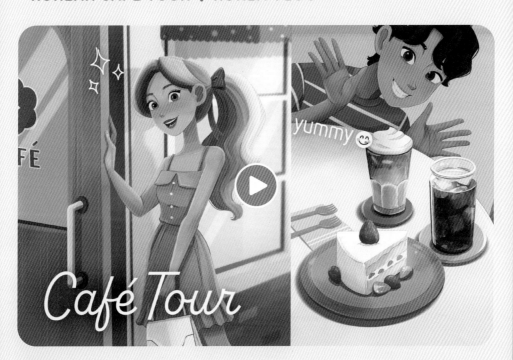

KOREAN CAFÉ TOUR | KOREA VLOG

yummy

Café Tour

 KATE

Learning Objective
#Ask_for_What_You_Want   #Customize_Your_Order_at_a_Café   #Sweeter_than_Sweet♪

Warm-up
Question

In a café, there are many other drinks besides coffee. Different people have different beverage preferences. Some members of BTS like coffee and some do not. What is your beverage preference?

안녕하세요. 케이트예요! 오늘은 슌 씨하고 카페에 왔어요.
Hi, I'm Kate! Today, I came to a café with Shun.

슌 씨, 카페가 정말 예뻐요. 그렇죠?
Shun, the café is really beautiful, isn't it?

(at the checkout counter)

음... 우리 뭐 마실까요? 저는 아이스 아메리카노 마시고 싶어요.
Hmm... What should we drink? I want to drink an iced Americano.

슌 씨는 뭐 마시고 싶어요?
What do you want to drink, Shun?

여러분은 보통 카페에서 뭐 마셔요?
What do you usually drink at a café?

추천해 주세요! 댓글에 써 주세요.
Give us your recommendations! Write them in the comments.

그럼 오늘 영상도 재미있게 봐 주세요. 😊
I hope you enjoy today's video too.

카페 메뉴 Café Menu

⊙ Here's the menu for the café that Kate and Shun went to. What is your favorite drink?

MENU

커피 Coffee (HOT/ICED)	R	L
에스프레소 Espresso	3.5	
아메리카노 Americano	4.5	5.0
카페라떼 Caffe Latte	5.0	5.5
카푸치노 Cappuccino	5.0	5.5

샷 추가 Extra shot +0.5
디카페인 변경 Change to decaf +0.5

* 샷 shot, 추가 add
   디카페인 decaffeine, 변경 change

차 Tea (HOT/ICED)	R	L
녹차 Green Tea	4.5	5.0
홍차 Black Tea	4.5	5.0
• 얼그레이 Earl Grey		
허브티 Herbal Tea	4.5	5.0
• 캐모마일 Chamomile		
• 페퍼민트 Peppermint		
유자차 Yuja Tea	5.5	6.0

음료 Drinks (HOT/ICED)	R	L
녹차라떼 Green Tea Latte	5.5	6.0
밀크티 Milk Tea	5.5	6.0
(iced only) 자몽에이드 Grapefruit Ade		6.0
(iced only) 생과일주스 Fresh Fruit Juice		6.5
• 딸기 Strawberry		
• 바나나 Banana		
• 키위 Kiwi		

디저트 Dessert	
아이스크림 Ice Cream	3.5
와플 Waffles	3.7
딸기 케이크 Strawberry Cake	6.5
치즈 케이크 Cheesecake	6.5
팥빙수 Pat-bing-su (Shaved Ice with Red Beans)	9.0

"." is used to represent thousands.
5.0 = 5,000원   0.5 = 500원

Tip!

When ordering a hot or cold drink, add the words below in front of the item.

HOT: 따뜻한 (warm)

ICED: 아이스 (iced), 차가운 (cold)

 Practice   Which drink would you recommend to Kate?

→ _____ 추천해요!

카페에서 At a Café

♧ There are a lot of different people at a café. What are they doing?

이야기하다 to talk

컵 cup

사진을 찍다 to take a picture

마시다 to drink

빨대 straw

빼다 to remove, to leave out

기다리다 to wait

주문하다 to order

추천하다 to recommend

시럽 syrup

넣다 to add

영수증 receipt

ICE

얼음 ice

만들다 to make

Practice Answer the following question in Korean.

케이트는 지금 뭐 해요?

Expression 1

Ⓥ verb

✧ EASY to Use!

You can use this expression to say that you want to do something.

e.g. 마시다, 먹다   고 싶다

→ 커피를 **마시**고 싶어요.
I want to drink coffee.

→ 케이크도 **먹**고 싶어요.
I also want to eat cake.

✧ EASY to Speak!

- 방탄소년단 콘서트에 가고 싶어요.
  I want to go to a BTS concert.

- 한국어로 이야기하고 싶어요.
  I want to talk in Korean.

- 어떤 선물을 받고 싶어요?
  What gift do you want to receive?

- A: 뭐 하고 싶어요?
  What do you want to do?
  B: 한국을 여행하고 싶어요.
  I want to travel around Korea.

Tip!

"보고 싶다." This is one of the most famous lyrics from BTS' "봄날 (Spring Day)." If you add "Ⓥ고 싶다" to "보다" (to see), it can be used to say that you miss someone or something.

아미, 보고 싶어요!
ARMY, we miss you!

Vocabulary

Ⓝ 케이크 cake • 한국어로 in Korean • 어떤 what • Ⓝ 선물 gift • Ⓝ 여행 travel • Ⓥ 여행하다 to travel

Practice

⊙ **More practice**   STEP 5

If you were to meet BTS, what would you like to do? Answer the question using the given words.

Q. 뭐 하고 싶어요?

| Example | 같이, 사진, 찍다 | → | 같이 사진을 찍고 싶어요 . |

1 같이, 이야기하다 → _____ .

2 사인, 받다 → _____ .

3 같이, 노래, 부르다 → _____ .

4 춤, 배우다 → _____ .

5 편지, 주다 → _____ .

6 Write your own answer. → _____ .

Ⓝ 사인 autograph **Ⓝ** 춤 dance **Ⓝ** 편지 letter

Expression 2

Ⅴ 아/어/해 주다

Ⅴ verb

✛ EASY to Use!

You can use this expression to describe an action that is done for someone. It can be combined with other expressions to be used in different situations. (e.g. "Ⅴ아/어/해 주세요," "Ⅴ아/어/해 줬어요," "Ⅴ아/어/해 줄까요?")

"ㅗ" or "ㅏ" before "다" (e.g. 보다)	⊕ 아 주다 →	오늘 영상 재미있게 **보**+주세요. ⊕(으)세요 Please enjoy today's video.
neither "ㅗ" nor "ㅏ" before "다" (e.g. 찍다)	⊕ 어 주다 →	슌 씨가 사진을 **찍**+어 줬어요. ⊕았/었/했어요 Shun took a picture for me.
"하" before "다" (e.g. 추천하다)	→ 해 주다	**추천해** 주세요. ⊕(으)세요 Please give me a recommendation.

✛ EASY to Speak!

- 친구가 밥을 사 줬어요.
  My friend bought me a meal.

- 잠시만 기다려 주세요.
  Please wait a moment.

- 영수증 버려 주세요.
  Please throw away the receipt.

- 답장해 주세요.
  Please reply.

- A: 가방 무겁지 않아요? 제가 들어 줄까요?
  Isn't your bag heavy? Should I carry it for you?

  B: 네, 감사합니다.
  Yes, thank you.

Tip!

When requesting help in an emergency situation, you can use "도와주다" (to help) as follows:

도와주세요!
Please help!

When you need to use honorifics to talk about an action done for someone else, you can use the expression "Ⅴ아/어/해 드리다."

가방 들어 드릴까요?
Should I carry the bag for you?

Vocabulary

- 재미있게 with enjoyment   • 잠시(잠시만) a moment   Ⅴ 버리다 to throw away   Ⅴ 답장하다 to reply
- Ⓐ 무겁다 to be heavy   Ⅴ 들다 to carry   Ⅴ 도와주다 to help

1. Complete the sentences by combining "☑️아/어/해 주다" with other expressions.

Example (알리다, -아/어/해 줬어요)	→	케이트 씨가 ___알려 줬어요___ .
❶ (소개하다, -아/어/해 줄까요?)	→	제 친구를 _____ ?
❷ (만들다, -아/어/해 줬어요)	→	생일 케이크를 _____ .
❸ (가르치다, -아/어/해 주세요)	→	이 단어 뜻을 _____ .
❹ (오다, -아/어/해 주세요)	→	파티에 _____ .

2. BTS is having a live performance. What do you think they will say? Complete the sentences using "☑️아/어/해 주세요" with the given words.

Example **우리 아미 여러분! 여기** 봐 주세요 **.** (보다)

새 앨범이 나왔어요!

❶ 많이 _____ . (듣다)

❷ 곧 콘서트도 해요. _____ . (기대하다)

❸ 조금만 _____ . (기다리다)

아미 여러분, 정말 보고 싶어요.

❹ 콘서트에도 많이 _____ . (오다)

❺ 그럼 이번 앨범도 많이 _____ . (사랑하다)

ᵥₒcₐbᵤₗₐᵣy

☑️ 알리다 to inform ☑️ 소개하다 to introduce 🅽 생일 birthday 🅽 뜻 meaning
☑️ 가르치다 to teach 🅽 파티 party • 새 new 🅽 앨범 album
☑️ 나오다 to be released ☑️ 기대하다 to be excited for • 조금만 just a little bit • 그럼 then
• 이번 this; this time ☑️ 사랑하다 to love

looking at the menu in a café

슌 씨, 뭐 마시고 싶어요?

음... 저는 아이스 밀크티 마시고 싶어요.
케이트 씨는 뭐가 당겨요?

저는 아이스 아메리카노요. 우리 딸기 케이크도 먹어요.

moves to the counter

안녕하세요. 아이스 아메리카노하고 아이스 밀크티 주세요.
딸기 케이크도 하나 주세요.

네, 만 육천오백 원입니다. 매장에서 드시고 가세요?

네. 그리고 밀크티는 시럽 반만 넣어 주세요.

네, 알겠습니다. 영수증 드릴까요?

아니요, 영수증은 버려 주세요.

vocabulary

V 당기다 to be in the mood for; to pull   **N** 매장 store   • 드시고 가세요? For here?   **N** 반 half   • 알겠습니다. Okay.

Practice

1. What did Kate and Shun order?

2. Which drink would you order if you went to the café? Write down your order and say it aloud.
   (See page 96 for the menu.)

메뉴 [✓] 아이스 [ ] 따뜻한 __녹차라떼__

Customize

얼음 [ ] 많이 넣다 [ ] 반만 넣다 [ ] 빼다
시럽 [ ] 많이 넣다 [✓] 반만 넣다 [ ] 빼다

[ ] 매장에서 먹고 가요 for here
[✓] 테이크 아웃 할게요 to go

메뉴 [ ] 아이스 [ ] 따뜻한 _____

Customize

얼음 [ ] 많이 넣다 [ ] 반만 넣다 [ ] 빼다
시럽 [ ] 많이 넣다 [ ] 반만 넣다 [ ] 빼다

[ ] 매장에서 먹고 가요 for here
[ ] 테이크 아웃 할게요 to go

아이스 녹차라떼 하나 주세요.
시럽은 반만 넣어 주세요. 테이크 아웃 할게요.

Real Korean

The food is pulling me in!

When you crave something, you can use
the expression "당기다" in conversations,
which literally means "to pull." In this case,
"당기다" is often pronounced as "땡기다."

- A: 저녁 뭐 먹을까요?
  What should we have for dinner?

  B: 음... 저는 치킨이 당겨요.
  Hmm... I'm in the mood for fried chicken.

Visit Korean cafés like a local!

In Korea, you can find cafés everywhere.
If you are familiar with the expressions below,
you will be able to order any drink you want!

- 키오스크에서 주문해 주세요.
  Please order at the kiosk.

- 더 필요하신 건 없으세요?
  Do you need anything else?

- 시럽/설탕/얼음 빼 주세요.
  No syrup/sugar/ice, please.

- A: 드시고 가세요? For here?
  B1: 네, 먹고 가요. Yes, for here, please.
  B2: 아니요, 테이크 아웃 할게요. No, to go, please.

- 조금만 기다려 주세요.
  Just a moment, please.

- 준비되면 불러 드릴게요.
  I'll call you when it's ready.

K-디저트를 아시나요?
Do You Know K-Desserts?

먹방 (mukbang) originated in Korea, so it is not very surprising that Koreans are very passionate about eating. From traditional to fusion desserts, here are some K-desserts that you must try when you come to Korea.

A typical traditional dessert is 약과 (*yak-gwa*). 약과 is made by mixing flour, sesame oil, and honey into a dough, cutting the dough into pretty shapes, and then frying it. It has a chewy texture and a sweet taste, making it quite an addictive dessert. Along with traditional 약과, there are many fusion desserts such as cookies and scones made with 약과.

Koreans love desserts from all parts of the world. Have you heard of 뚱카롱 (뚱뚱한 마카롱, thick macarons)? Macarons usually have a thin layer of cream in the middle. However, Korean macarons are made with generous amounts of cream, and even contain fruits, cookies, and more. With their larger size, you can experience richer flavors and textures!

Do you know any pretty cafés?
Make a vlog where you introduce a café and place an order.

"오늘은 친구하고 카페에 왔어요. 우리 뭐 마실까요? ..."

Episode 8 주말 나들이 (Feat. 서울)

WEEKEND OUTING (FEAT. SEOUL) | KOREA VLOG

 KATE

Learning Objective

#Talk_about_Plans   #Happy_Weekend

Warm-up
Question

When BTS has some free time, they sometimes visit art galleries or museums, meet up with friends, or go on a little outing for a change of scenery.
How about you? What do you like to do in your free time?

At the National Museum of Korea

안녕하세요. 케이트예요! 저 주말에 진짜 바빠요!
Hi, I'm Kate! I'm really busy this weekend!

이번 주 토요일에 친구들하고 놀이공원에 갈 거예요.
I'm going to an amusement park with some friends this Saturday.

그 놀이공원은 〈달려라 방탄〉에 나왔어요.
The amusement park was featured in 〈Run BTS!〉.

저는 놀이기구를 진짜진짜 좋아해요. 놀이기구를 정말 많이 탈 거예요.
I really, really like rides. I'm going to ride a lot of rides.

일요일에는 슌 씨하고 경복궁에 갈 거예요.
On Sunday, I'm going to Gyeongbokgung Palace with Shun.

한복을 입고 경복궁에 들어갈 거예요.
We'll wear hanbok and visit Gyeongbokgung Palace.

사진도 많이 찍을 거예요.
We'll take a lot of pictures.

예전부터 경복궁에 정말 가고 싶었어요. 그래서 너무 기대돼요.
I've always wanted to go to Gyeongbokgung Palace. So I'm really excited about it.

Vocabulary

⊙ **Learn the vocabulary** STEP 2

장소와 행동 Places and Activities

♧ Here are some places to go for a weekend outing. Let's see what Kate and Shun are up to.

출구
exit

(지하철)역
(subway) station

지하철
subway

타다
to take

놀이공원
amusement park

놀이기구를 타다
to go on rides

입구
entrance

응원하다
to cheer

공연장
concert venue

표를 사다
to buy a ticket

매표소
ticket office

관람하다
to see, to visit

박물관
museum

한복 대여점
hanbok rental shop

한복
hanbok

빌리다
to rent

입다
to wear

경복궁
Gyeongbokgung Palace

구경하다
to look around

서점
bookstore

Practice Where would you like to go this weekend?

→ _____ 에 가고 싶어요.

날짜 Date

◇ To say the date in Korean, the Chinese character numbers (일, 이, 삼, ... → see page 37) are used. Months are called "월," and days are called "일." You can use "몇 월 며칠" (what month and day) or "언제" (when) to ask about dates.

일월 January	이월 February	삼월 March	사월 April	오월 May	유월 June
칠월 July	팔월 August	구월 September	시월 October	십일월 November	십이월 December

일 일 1st	이 일 2nd	삼 일 3rd	사 일 4th	···	삼십일 일 31st

6월

주말 weekend

월요일 Monday	화요일 Tuesday	수요일 Wednesday	목요일 Thursday	금요일 Friday	토요일 Saturday	일요일 Sunday	
		1	2 시험 ☑	3	4		
5	6		9	10	11		지난주 last week
12	13 어제 yesterday 방탄소년단 데뷔일 BTS' debut date	14 오늘 today	15 내일 tomorrow	16	17 놀이공원 🎡	18 경복궁 📷	이번 주 this week
19	20	21	22	23 생일 🎂	24	25	다음 주 next week

> 오늘은 유월 십사 일 수요일이에요.
> Today is Wednesday, June 14.

Practice Answer the following questions in Korean.

1. 케이트는 유월 십칠 일에 놀이공원에 가요. 언제 경복궁에 가요?

2. 방탄소년단 데뷔일은 몇 월 며칠이에요?

3. 오늘은 몇 월 며칠이에요? (Answer based on where you are.)

V (으)ㄹ 거예요

V verb

⬦ EASY to Use!

You can use this expression to talk about a plan or your determination to do something.

| with batchim before "다" (excluding "ㄹ") (e.g. 찍다) | ➕ 을 거예요 | → | 사진을 을 거예요.
I am going to take a picture. |

| without batchim or with batchim "ㄹ" before "다" ("ㄹ" is dropped) (e.g. 가다, 놀다) | ➕ ㄹ 거예요 | ↗ | 놀이공원에 거예요.
I am going to the amusement park. |
| | | ↘ | 친구하고 거예요.
I am going to hang out with my friend. |

⬦ EASY to Speak!

- 한복을 입을 거예요.
  I am going to wear a hanbok.

- 미술관을 관람할 거예요.
  I am going to visit an art museum.

- 방탄소년단 노래를 들을 거예요.   [듣다 Irregular Conjugation (p. 167)]
  I am going to listen to BTS songs.

- A : 이번 주 토요일에 뭐 해요?
  What are you doing this Saturday?

- B : 백화점에 갈 거예요. 거기에서 옷을 살 거예요.
  I am going to the department store.
  I am going to buy clothes there.

Tip!

"-(으)ㄹ 거예요" can also be used to express the speaker's guess or opinion. Both adjectives and verbs can be used.

내일 날씨가 좋을 거예요.
The weather will be nice tomorrow.

지하철이 더 편할 거예요.
You will be more comfortable on the subway.

1. What will you do when you have free time? Complete the sentences using the given words.

Example 집에서 쉬다

방탄소년단 영상을 보다

집에서 쉴 거예요 . _____ .

2 놀이공원에서 놀다

3 서점에서 책을 읽다

4 your own answer

_____ . _____ . _____ .

2. Here is Shun's schedule for next week. Answer the questions.

	월요일	화요일	수요일	목요일	금요일	토요일	일요일
수업		한강공원 자전거 🚲 타다		박물관 🏛 관람하다	생일 케이크 🎂 만들다	방탄소년단 춤 🕺 배우다	

Example Q. 다음 주 화요일에 뭐 해요?

A. 한강공원에서 자전거를 탈 거예요 .

1 Q. 다음 주 목요일에 뭐 해요?

A. _____ .

2 Q. 다음 주 금요일에 뭐 해요?

A. _____ .

3 Q. 다음 주 토요일에 뭐 해요?

A. _____ .

> **A/V** adjective or verb
> **V** verb

⬦ EASY to Use!

You can use this expression to list actions or different qualities of something. You can also use this expression to list actions in a chronological order.

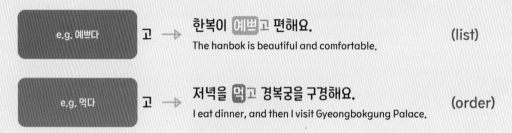

e.g. 예쁘다	고 →	한복이 **예쁘**고 편해요. The hanbok is beautiful and comfortable.	(list)
e.g. 먹다	고 →	저녁을 **먹**고 경복궁을 구경해요. I eat dinner, and then I visit Gyeongbokgung Palace.	(order)

⬦ EASY to Speak!

- 음식이 싸고 맛있어요.
  The food is cheap and delicious.

- 카페에서 커피도 마시고 책도 읽어요.
  I drink coffee and read books in cafés.

- 영화를 보고 쇼핑을 했어요.
  I saw a movie and went shopping.

- A : 어제 뭐 했어요?
  What did you do yesterday?

- B : 머스터*에 갔어요. 공연도 보고 열심히 응원했어요.
  I went to the MUSTER. I watched the performances and cheered really hard.

*머스터 (MUSTER): the name of BTS' fan meetings

Tip!

"**A/V**고" is often used like this:
"**N**도 **A/V**고 **N**도 **A/V**아/어/해요."

친구하고 같이 게임도 하고 노래방도 갔어요.
I played games and went to the *noraebang* with my friend.

If you use "**V**고" after some verbs such as "입다" (to wear) and "타다" (to ride), it can indicate that the second action occurs while the result of the first action still remains.

한복을 입고 사진을 찍었어요.
I wore a hanbok and took a picture.

버스를 타고 놀이공원에 갈 거예요.
I am going to take the bus to the amusement park.

vocabulary

N 음식 food **N** 쇼핑 shopping **N** 공연 performance **N** 버스 bus

1. Complete the sentences by listing the given actions or qualities.

Example　재미있다, 감동적이었다　⟶　영화가 ___재미있고 감동적이었어요___ .

1　노래도 부르다, 응원도 했다　⟶　공연장에서 _____ .

2　노래도 잘하다, 춤도 잘 추다　⟶　방탄소년단은 _____ .

3　표를 사다, 박물관에 들어가다　⟶　_____ .

4　축구를 하다, 점심을 먹었다　⟶　_____ .

2. This is Kate's Saturday diary entry. Complete the sentences using the given words.

오늘 놀이공원에 갔어요.

Example　놀이공원에서 _교복을 입고_ 놀이기구를 탔어요. (교복, 입다)

1　놀이공원이 진짜 _____ 예뻤어요. (넓다)

2　친구들하고 _____ 간식도 많이 먹었어요. (사진, 찍다)

3　그리고 _____ 집에 왔어요. (지하철, 타다)

내일은 숲 씨하고 경복궁에 갈 거예요.

4　먼저 _____ 한복을 빌릴 거예요. (저녁, 먹다)

내일도 너무 기대돼요.

 슌 씨, 벌써 토요일이에요! 우리 내일 몇 시에 볼까요?

 음... 오후 6시 어때요? 같이 저녁 먹고 경복궁 구경해요.

네, 좋아요! 그럼 어디에서 만날까요?
경복궁 역 4번 출구 앞 어때요?

 네, 그래요. ㅎㅎ

우리 한복은 어디에서 빌릴 거예요?

 4번 출구 근처에 한복 대여점이 많이 있어요.
먼저 저녁 먹고 거기에서 한복 빌려요. 그리고 경복궁에 가요.

와, 벌써 두근거리고 기대돼요. ㅋㅋ 😄 그럼 내일 봐요!

 저도요. ㅎㅎㅎ 내일 봐요!

• 벌써 already N 번 No. N 근처 vicinity V 두근거리다 to pound

114

Practice

1. What are Kate and Shun going to do tomorrow? List the events in order. [　]→[　]→[　]→[　]

   A 한복을 빌릴 거예요.　　**B** 경복궁을 구경할 거예요.　　**C** 경복궁 역에서 만날 거예요.　　**D** 저녁을 먹을 거예요.

2. Did you know that there are many BTS-related spots in Seoul? If you were in Seoul, where would you go over the weekend? What would you do there?

경복궁
Gyeongbokgung Palace

학동공원
Hakdong Park

놀이공원
amusement park

국립중앙박물관
National Museum of Korea

저는 국립중앙박물관에 가고 싶어요.
거기에서 방탄소년단이 노래를 불렀어요.
저는 국립중앙박물관에서 사진을 찍고
박물관도 구경할 거예요.

저는 _____

_____

_____

Real Korean

Talk like a native Korean speaker using omission

In real-life conversations, "이/가" and "을/를," which indicate the subject or object, respectively, and "에," which indicates the destination of movement, are often omitted. Though they are used in formal settings and in writing, it is much more natural to omit them when speaking.

Look for these omissions In Kate and Shun's conversation! (See page 114)

● 같이 저녁(을) 먹고 경복궁(을) 구경해요.

Laugh with letters ㅋㅋㅋㅋㅋ

When sending text messages, you can use consonants alone to express different meanings. But just remember that this is usually used only between people who have a close relationship.

● ㄱㄱ (고고, go go)
  "Let's go!"

● ㄴㄴ (노노, no no)
  "No."

● ㄷㄷ (덜덜)
  (shivering)

● ㅇㅇ (응응)
  "Yes."

● ㅋㅋ or ㅎㅎ
  (laughing)

● ㅇㅋ (오케이, okay)
  "Okay, great."

● ㅊㅋㅊㅋ (축하축하[추카추카])
  (congratulating someone)

한복 입고 경복궁 구경하기
Visit Gyeongbokgung Palace Wearing a Hanbok

There are many BTS-related spots in Seoul, Korea. Let's take a look at one of them, 경복궁 (Gyeongbokgung Palace).

'Dynamite' Stage CAM (BTS focus) @ Gyeongbokgung

In 2020, BTS performed "Dynamite," "IDOL," and "소우주 (Mikrokosmos)" at Gyeongbokgung Palace. With the old palace built about 600 years ago as the backdrop, BTS' remarkable performance was broadcast around the world. BTS wore elegant outfits that included elements of 한복 (hanbok) that enhanced their already stunning performance. If you are ARMY who watched this performance, you will want to visit Gyeongbokgung Palace.

Wearing a hanbok when you visit Gyeongbokgung Palace is highly recommended. There are many hanbok rental shops in the area. Wearing a hanbok is a great way not only to take unique photos but also to experience Korean culture. Plus, if you are wearing a hanbok, admission to Gyeongbokgung Palace is free of charge. You can also visit Gyeongbokgung Palace at night, which is a whole different experience from the daytime. However, it is only open at night during certain periods in spring and fall, so be sure to check the exact dates before visiting. (For more information, check out 〈BTS TRAVEL BOOK〉!)

Create Your Own Vlog

Make a vlog talking about your weekend plans.

"저 주말에 진짜 바빠요! 이번 주 토요일에 …"

Episode 9

한국에서 즐기는 취미 생활

HOBBIES TO ENJOY IN KOREA | KOREA VLOG

My Hobbies

 KATE

Learning Objective

#Hobbies_and_Feelings   #Because_It_Is_Fun   #BTS_Dance_Class

Warm-up

Warm-up
Question

BTS' incredible choreography makes us want
to challenge ourselves to dance like them!
Is there any BTS choreography that you can
dance? What would you like to learn?
(Quiz! Guess which songs the choreographies above are from!)

안녕하세요. 슌이에요! 오늘은 제가 케이트 씨 브이로그를 찍을 거예요.
Hi. I'm Shun! Today, I'll be filming for Kate's vlog.

방탄소년단 춤을 배우고 싶어서 케이트 씨하고 댄스 학원에 왔어요.
I came to a dance academy with Kate because I wanted to learn BTS dances.

근데 케이트 씨가 춤을 진짜 잘 춰서 깜짝 놀랐어요.
By the way, I was surprised by what a good dancer Kate is.

 케이트 씨, 힘들지 않아요?
Kate, aren't you tired?

너무 재미있어서 하나도 안 힘들어요.
I'm having too much fun, so I'm not tired at all.

숀 씨, 우리 같이 댄스 커버 영상 찍을까요?
Shun, should we film a dance cover video together?

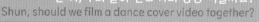

 네? 😮 아니에요. 저는 춤을 못 춰서…
What? No, I can't dance, so…

에이, 숀 씨도 할 수 있어요! 이쪽으로 와요.
Oh come on. You can do it too! Come here.

먼저 스트레칭 할까요? 하나, 둘, 셋, …
Should we stretch first? One, two, three, …

 하나, 둘, 으악! 😣
One, two, ouch!

취미 Hobbies

⟳ Kate's hobby is dancing, and she is a great dancer. What do you think Shun's hobby is?

요리를 하다
to cook

수영을 하다
to swim

기타를 치다
to play the guitar

테니스를 치다
to play tennis

노래를 부르다
to sing a song

춤을 추다
to do a dance

자전거를 타다
to ride a bicycle

제 취미는 요리예요.
My hobby is cooking.

Tip!
When you say it like this, you need to use only the noun.

저는 춤추는 것을 좋아해요.
I love to dance.

자전거 타는 것도 좋아해요!
I also love to ride a bicycle!

Tip!
When you say it like this, change the vocabulary as below:

춤(을) 추(다) → 춤추는 것
자전거(를) 타(다) → 자전거 타는 것

Practice   Answer the following question in Korean.

여러분은 취미가 뭐예요?

능력 Ability

♢ You can use the words below to express your level of ability.

못하다 (못 V)	잘 못하다 (잘 못 V)	잘하다 (잘 V)
I cannot do it. I am not good at it.	I can do it, but I am not really good at it.	I can do it. I am good at it.

Practice Answer the following question in Korean.

여러분은 한국어를 잘해요?

느낌 Feelings

♢ Kate is having fun dancing. Shun is surprised by her dancing skills. You can use the words below to express your different thoughts and feelings.

즐겁다
to be joyful

힘들다
to be tired

무섭다
to be scared

피곤하다
to be exhausted

놀라다
to be surprised

기쁘다
to be happy

슬프다
to be sad

궁금하다
to be curious

자신 있다
to be confident
자신 없다
to not be confident

긴장되다
to be nervous

Practice How would you feel in the following situations? Answer in Korean.

① 방탄소년단 콘서트에 왔어요. 콘서트가 곧 시작해요!

② 하루 종일 일했어요.

Ⓥ (으)ㄹ 수 있다[없다]

Ⓥ verb

✧ EASY to Use!

You can use "Ⓥ(으)ㄹ 수 있다" to say that you have the ability to do something or to say that something is possible. When you do not have the ability to do something or when something is impossible, you can use "Ⓥ(으)ㄹ 수 없다."

with batchim before "다" (excluding "ㄹ") (e.g. 읽다)	⊕ 을 수 있다[없다]	→	한글을 읽을 수 있어요.

I can read Hangeul.

without batchim or with batchim "ㄹ" before "다" ("ㄹ" is dropped) (e.g. 하다, 들다)	⊕ ㄹ 수 있다[없다]	→	수영을 할 수 있어요.

I can swim.

가방을 들 수 없어요.
I cannot carry the bag.

✧ EASY to Speak!

- 지금 전화를 받을 수 없어요.
  I cannot answer the phone right now.

- 기타를 칠 수 있어요.
  I can play the guitar.

- 다리가 아파요. 걸을 수 없어요.   ┤걷다 Irregular Conjugation (p. 167)├
  My leg hurts. I cannot walk.

- A : 한국 음식을 만들 수 있어요?
  Can you make Korean food?

  B : 네. 닭갈비하고 김치볶음밥을 만들 수 있어요.
  Yes. I can make *dak-gal-bi* and *kimchi bo-kkeum-bap*.

Tip!

Instead of using "Ⓥ(으)ㄹ 수 없다," which indicates an inability or impossibility, you can also use "못 Ⓥ."

읽을 수 있어요. ↔ 읽을 수 없어요.
= 못 읽어요.
I cannot read it.

Ⓝ 한글 Hangeul   Ⓝ 다리 leg(s)   Ⓐ 아프다 to be hurt   Ⓝ 닭갈비 *dak-gal-bi* (spicy stir-fried chicken)

Practice

Complete both answers, and check the box that applies to you.

Example

자전거를 탈 수 있어요?

☑ 네, 탈 수 있어요.

☐ 아니요, 탈 수 없어요.

1

〈Dynamite〉 춤을 출 수 있어요?

☐ 네, _____.

☐ 아니요, _____.

2

〈Life Goes On〉 노래를 부를 수 있어요?

☐ 네, _____.

☐ 아니요, _____.

3

불닭을 먹을 수 있어요?

☐ 네, _____.

☐ 아니요, _____.

vocabulary

N 불닭 *bul-dak* (very spicy stir-fried chicken)

A/V 아/어/해서

A/V adjective or verb

⟡ EASY to Use!

You can use this expression to state the cause or reason of the latter part of the sentence.

| "ㅗ" or "ㅏ" before "다"
(e.g. 작다) | ⊕ 아서 → | 신발이 작아서 불편해요.
My shoes are small, so they are uncomfortable. |

| neither "ㅗ" nor "ㅏ"
before "다"
(e.g. 힘들다) | ⊕ 어서 → | 힘들어서 잠깐 쉬었어요.
I was tired, so I rested for a moment. |

| "하" before "다"
(e.g. 좋아하다) | → 해서 → | 춤을 좋아해서 매일 연습해요.
I like dancing, so I practice every day. |

⟡ EASY to Speak!

- 핸드폰이 고장 나서 연락할 수 없었어요.
  My cell phone stopped working, so I could not contact you.

- 늦어서 죄송해요.
  I am sorry for being late.

- 테니스를 배우고 싶어서 테니스 수업을 신청했어요.
  I wanted to learn tennis, so I signed up for a tennis class.

- 한국어를 너무 잘해서 깜짝 놀랐어요.
  Your Korean was very good, so I was surprised.

- 목이 아파서 노래를 부를 수 없어요. | "ㅡ" Elimination (p. 167) |
  My throat hurts, so I cannot sing.

- A : 왜 한국어를 배워요?
  Why are you learning Korean?

- B : 방탄소년단을 좋아해서요. (=방탄소년단을 좋아해서 한국어를 배워요.)
  Because I like BTS.

Tip!

When most verbs and adjectives with batchim "ㅂ" before "다," like "즐겁다," are combined with an expression that begins with a vowel, the "ㅂ" changes to "ㅜ." (See page 167)

즐겁다 + 어서 → 즐거우어서 → 즐거워서
무섭다 + 어서 → 무서우어서 → 무서워서
맵다 + 어서 → 매우어서 → 매워서

ⓥⓞⓒⓐⓑⓤⓛⓐⓡⓨ

- N 신발 shoes
- 잠깐 a moment
- 매일 every day
- V 연습하다 to practice
- 고장(이) 나다 to stop working
- V 연락하다 to contact
- V 늦다 to arrive late
- A 죄송하다 to be sorry
- V 신청하다 to sign up for
- 깜짝 놀라다 to be startled
- N 목 throat; neck
- 왜 why
- A 맵다 to be spicy

Practice

1. Complete the sentences using the given words and "A/V 아/어/해서."

| Example | 야채튀김이 맛있다 | → | <u>야채튀김이 맛있어서</u> | 하나 더 먹었어요. |

❶ 일이 많다 → _____ 약속에 못 가요.

❷ 영화가 무섭다 → _____ 잘 볼 수 없었어요.

❸ 조금 피곤하다 → _____ 자고 싶어요.

❹ 한국어를 잘하고 싶다 → _____ 케이크 앱 강의를 들어요.

2. You are talking about why you are learning Korean. Answer the question.

Q. 왜 한국어를 배워요?

한국어가 재미있다

__한국어가 재미있어서요__ .

방탄소년단 영상을 자막 없이 보고 싶다

_____ .

방탄소년단 노래 가사를 잘 알고 싶다

_____ .

your own answer

_____ .

Dialogue

⊙ Listen and practice speaking   STEP 8

after learning a dance

 K-POP 댄스 클래스 정말 즐거웠어요.
케이트 씨는 여기 자주 와요?

네, 춤을 좋아해서 자주 와요. 슌 씨는 취미가 뭐예요?

 저는 요리하는 것을 좋아해요.
그래서 집에서 요리를 자주 해요.

와, 멋있어요. 저 슌 씨 요리 너무 궁금해요!

 마침 다음 주말에 한국 요리 쿠킹 클래스에 가요.
케이트 씨도 같이 가요!

저도 배울 수 있어요? 저는 요리를 잘 못해서 자신 없어요.

 괜찮아요. 케이트 씨도 할 수 있어요. 저만 믿어요.

하하, 그래요. 슌 씨가 잘 가르쳐 주세요.

Vocabulary

ℕ 댄스 클래스 dance class ・ 자주 often ・ 마침 happen to be, happen to have ℕ 쿠킹 클래스 cooking class
Ⓐ 괜찮다 to be okay Ⓥ 믿다 to trust, to believe

Practice

1. What is Shun's hobby? Where are Kate and Shun going next weekend?

2. What do you want to learn? Imagine you are applying for a class. Write an application like the one below.

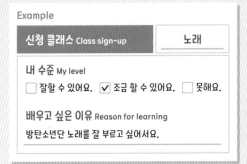

Example

| 신청 클래스 Class sign-up | 노래 |

내 수준 My level
☐ 잘할 수 있어요. ☑ 조금 할 수 있어요. ☐ 못해요.

배우고 싶은 이유 Reason for learning
방탄소년단 노래를 잘 부르고 싶어서요.

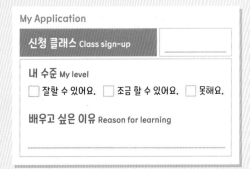

My Application

| 신청 클래스 Class sign-up | |

내 수준 My level
☐ 잘할 수 있어요. ☐ 조금 할 수 있어요. ☐ 못해요.

배우고 싶은 이유 Reason for learning

Real Korean

"항상" love you, ARMY

When you want to indicate the frequency of something, try saying this!

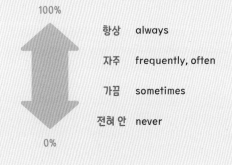

100%

항상	always
자주	frequently, often
가끔	sometimes
전혀 안	never

0%

- A : 노래방에 자주 가요?
  Do you go to *noraebang* often?
  B : 네, 노래를 좋아해서 자주 가요.
  Yes, I go often because I like singing.

The all-purpose expression "괜찮아요!"

Have you ever heard the phrase "괜찮아" in BTS songs? "괜찮다" means many different things.

1 When something is not a problem
- 일이 많아요. 하지만 괜찮아요.
  I have a lot of work. But it's okay.

2 When the condition of something is not bad
- A : 이 옷 어때요?
  How is this outfit?
  B : 디자인이 괜찮아요.
  The design is not bad.

3 When refusing something politely
- A : 조금 더 드세요.
  Have some more food.
  B : 괜찮아요.
  I'm okay.

원데이 클래스 체험하기
Taking a One-Day Class

[BTS VLOG] SUGA | 목공방 VLOG

[BTS VLOG] Jimin | 팔찌공방 VLOG

K-pop dance, Korean cuisine, jewelry making, pottery, perfume mixing, woodworking, leatherworking, etc. ... In Korea, there are a lot of one-day classes where you can learn how to do different things. BTS has also taken one-day classes.

Jimin, who has a lot of interest in accessories, once went to a workshop and made a bracelet. He sawed and hammered the bracelet into shape and polished the surface to a shiny finish! Jimin was so pleased with the results that he recommended that ARMY try the bracelet workshop as well. SUGA, who loves furniture, went to a woodshop and made a cute whale-shaped cutting board. Though he only had a short amount of time, he carefully cut and refined the wood, and made seven cutting boards as gifts for the other members.

Did watching BTS' one-day class vlogs inspire you to try something new? One-day classes are a simple yet great way to make memories. If you are coming to Korea, why not challenge yourself to something new like Kate and Shun? Taking a cultural-experience class that is only available in Korea would be even better!

Create Your Own Vlog

Make a vlog showing yourself enjoying a hobby and explaining it in Korean.

"오늘은 OO을 배우고 싶어서 OO에 왔어요. ..."

Episode 10

한국 옷 가게에서 쇼핑하기

SHOPPING AT A KOREAN CLOTHING STORE | KOREA VLOG

#쇼핑 #OOTD

Shop With Me

 KATE

Learning Objective

#Go_Shopping   #Give_Suggestions_to_Try_Something   #Shop_With_Me

Warm-up
Question

From glamorous stage outfits to unique daily outfits, BTS fashion always hits the spot for ARMY. Which is your favorite style?

안녕하세요. 케이트예요! 오늘은 슌 씨하고 쇼핑몰에 왔어요.
Hi, I'm Kate! Today I came to the shopping mall with Shun.

저는 바지를 사고 슌 씨는 재킷을 살 거예요.
I'll buy a pair of pants, and Shun will buy a jacket.

여기 예쁜 옷들이 많아요! 😄
There are lots of pretty clothes here!

와, 이 보라색 티셔츠 좀 봐요. 너무 귀여워요!
Wow, look at this purple T-shirt. It's so cute!

이 노란색 원피스도 정말 예뻐요. 한번 입어 볼까요?
This yellow dress is really pretty. Should I try it on?

대박. 이 치마도 보세요. 이거 완전 제 옷이에요!
Whoa! Look at this skirt. This is totally mine!

여기 디자인이 멋진 모자도 있어요.
Here's a hat with a cool design.

어떡하죠? 다 사고 싶어요.
What should I do? I want to buy them all.

 **Vocabulary**

색 Colors

✛ What were the colors of the clothes that Kate saw? Say the different colors in Korean.

빨간색
red

주황색
orange

노란색
yellow

초록색
green

하늘색
light blue,
sky blue

파란색
blue

남색
dark blue,
navy blue

보라색
purple, violet

분홍색
pink

베이지색
beige

갈색
brown

하얀색, 흰색
white

검은색
black

회색
gray

 Practice Answer the following questions in Korean.

1. 여러분은 어떤 색을 좋아해요?

2. 여러분은 어떤 색 옷을 자주 입어요?

Tip!

By using "어떤" (which), you can ask about something specific or ask someone to choose among many options.

어떤 노래를 많이 들어요?
Which song do you listen to a lot?

어떤 색을 좋아해요?
Which color do you like?

옷 Clothes

⟡ In a clothing store, you can see many different types of clothes. In Korean, the word for "wear" changes depending on the type of clothing.

원피스 dress
티셔츠 T-shirt
셔츠 shirt
카디건 cardigan
재킷 jacket
입다 to wear
반바지 shorts
바지 pants
긴바지 long pants
청바지 jeans
치마 skirt
코트 coat
신발 shoes
구두 dress shoes
신다 to put on
쓰다 to put on
마스크 mask
모자 hat
양말 socks
운동화 sneakers
선글라스 sunglasses
안경 glasses
벗다 to take off

Practice Look at the picture above and fill in the blanks below.

❶ 숲은 _____ 재킷을 입어요.　❷ 케이트는 하얀색 _____ 을/를 신어요.

❸ 케이트는 _____ 을/를 써요.

▶ **Listen to the lecture with BTS**

STEP 4

A adjective
N noun

✧ EASY to Use!

This expression includes an adjective that modifies the noun that follows.

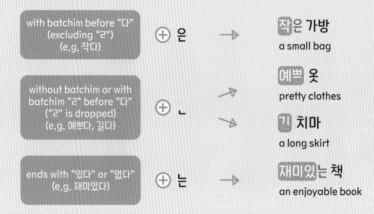

with batchim before "다"
(excluding "ㄹ")
(e.g. 작다)
⊕ 은 → 작은 가방
a small bag

without batchim or with
batchim "ㄹ" before "다"
("ㄹ" is dropped)
(e.g. 예쁘다, 길다)
⊕ ㄴ → 예쁜 옷
pretty clothes

긴 치마
a long skirt

ends with "있다" or "없다"
(e.g. 재미있다)
⊕ 는 → 재미있는 책
an enjoyable book

✧ EASY to Speak!

- 좋은 노래를 추천해 주세요.
  Please recommend a good song.

- 편한 운동화를 샀어요.
  I bought a pair of comfortable sneakers.

- 요즘 힘든 일 있어요?
  Is there something worrying you these days?

- 맛없는 음식을 먹고 싶지 않아요.
  I do not want to eat food that tastes bad.

- A : 어떤 옷 찾으세요?
  What clothes are you looking for?

- B : 가벼운 봄 재킷 있어요? ┤ ㅂ Irregular Conjugation (p. 167) ⟩
  Do you have a light spring jacket?

A 길다 to be long   N 요즘 nowadays   N 일 something   A 맛없다 to not be tasty   V 찾다 to look for

A 가볍다 to be light   N 봄 spring

134

Practice

⊙ **More practice** STEP 5

1. Imagine you are shopping at a clothing store. Use the given words to say what you need.

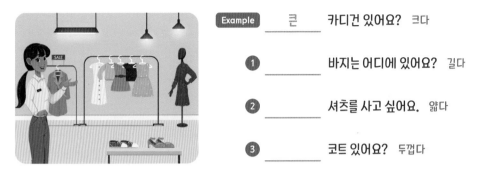

| Example | 큰 | 카디건 있어요? | 크다 |

1. _____ 바지는 어디에 있어요? 길다

2. _____ 셔츠를 사고 싶어요. 얇다

3. _____ 코트 있어요? 두껍다

2. How would you describe BTS' charm? Use the given words, or your own words, to describe BTS.

A
좋다   멋있다   매력적이다
감동적이다   인기 많다

⊕

N
노래   랩   춤
가사   가수   아이돌

Good music, good team?

Example
좋은 노래

Example
멋있는 춤

V o c a b u l a r y

Ⓐ 얇다 to be thin Ⓐ 두껍다 to be thick Ⓐ 매력적이다 to be charming • 인기(가) 많다 to be popular Ⓝ 랩 rap
Ⓝ 아이돌 idol

☑ 아/어/해 보다

☑ verb

✧ EASY to Use!

This expression means "to try a certain action." It can be combined with other expressions to be used in different situations. (e.g. "☑아/어/해 보세요," "☑아/어/해 볼까요?," "☑아/어/해 보고 싶어요.")

"ㅗ" or "ㅏ" before "다" (e.g. 가다)	⊕ 아 보다 →	한강공원에 **가** 보세요. ⊕ (으)세요 Try visiting Hangang Park.
neither "ㅗ" nor "ㅏ" before "다" (e.g. 입다)	⊕ 어 보다 →	한번 **입**어 보세요. ⊕ (으)세요 Try wearing it.
"하" before "다" (e.g. 시작하다)	→ 해 보다 →	**시작해** 볼까요? ⊕ (으)ㄹ까요? Should we get started?

✧ EASY to Speak!

- 맛집을 찾아 볼까요?
  Should we try to find some popular restaurants?

- 여기에서 사진을 찍어 보세요.
  Try taking a photo here.

- 아침 운동을 해 보세요.
  Try doing morning workouts.

- 〈둘! 셋!〉을 들어 보세요. ┤듣다 Irregular Conjugation (p. 167)├
  Try listening to "2! 3!"

- A : 한국 음식을 만들어 보고 싶어요.
  I want to try making Korean food.

  B : 저도요. 같이 배워 볼까요?
  Me too. Should we try to learn together?

> **Tip!**
>
> "☑아/어/해 보세요" is often used with "한번." Here, "한번" does not mean "once," but means "to give something a go."
>
> 한번 해 보세요.
> Try having a go.

Vocabulary

N 맛집 a popular restaurant

1. Complete the sentences by combining "✔아/어/해 보다" with other expressions.

Example (타다, -아/어/해 볼 거예요)   →   놀이기구를 ___타 볼 거예요___ .

❶ (구경하다, -아/어/해 볼까요?)   →   한번 _____?

❷ (가다, -아/어/해 보고 싶어요)   →   방탄소년단 콘서트에 _____.

❸ (읽다, -아/어/해 보세요)   →   댓글을 _____.

❹ (생각하다, -아/어/해 보세요)   →   다시 한번 _____.

2. Imagine you are a salesperson at a clothing store talking to a customer. Match each item to the correct word and complete the sentences using "한번 ✔아/어/해 보세요."

Example	• ————————— • 입다	**Example** 한번 입어 보세요 .
❶	• • 쓰다	❶ _____ .
❷	• • 입다	❷ _____ .
❸	• • 신다	❸ _____ .

Dialogue

FITTING ROOM

🔘 숀 씨, 이 바지 어때요?

🔘 와, 잘 어울려요.

🔘 그렇죠? 보라색이 예뻐서 저도 마음에 들어요.

🔘 음... 근데 조금 크지 않아요?

🔘 그래요? 한 사이즈 작은 것도 입어 볼까요?

(to a salesperson) 저기요. 혹시 이 바지 스몰(Small) 사이즈 있어요?

🔘 네, 잠시만요. 가져다드릴게요.

🔘 감사합니다.

(after buying the pants)

🔘 이제 숀 씨 재킷 같이 찾아 볼까요?

🔘 네, 좋아요. 저쪽에 ...

🔘 어? 숀 씨, 이 분홍색 원피스 보세요. 너무 예뻐요!

🔘 아, 네. 원피스도 입어 보세요, 하하. 😄

- **V** 어울리다 to suit
- 그렇죠? I know, right?
- 마음에 들다 to like
- **N** 사이즈 size
- **N** 것 that; one
- 저기요. Excuse me.
- 혹시 by any chance
- 잠시만요. One moment, please.
- 가져다드릴게요. I will get it for you.
- 이제 now

138

Practice Imagine you went to the clothing store on page 133.

1. Which clothes do you want to try on? Draw a clothing item you chose and talk about why you chose it.

 저는 이 긴 치마를 입어 보고 싶어요.
디자인이 예뻐서 마음에 들어요.

2. How about recommending some clothes to BTS? Draw a clothing item you would like to recommend and explain why you chose it.

 이 파란색 재킷을 입어 보세요.
잘 어울려서 추천해 주고 싶어요.

Real Korean

Shop like a local in Korean clothing stores!

These are some of the most common expressions used by salespeople. If you know these phrases, you will not have to worry about shopping in Korea.

- 찾으시는 거 있으세요?
  Are you looking for something?
- 필요한 거 있으시면 말씀해 주세요.
  Let me know if you need anything.
- 피팅룸은 저쪽에 있어요.
  The fitting room is over there.
- 그 옷은 피팅이 안 돼요.
  Those clothes are not available for trying on.
- 가져다드릴게요.
  I will get it for you.
- 계산 이쪽에서 도와드릴게요.
  You can pay for your items over here.

By any chance... do you know "혹시"?

When you need to ask someone something cautiously or ask them for a favor, add "혹시" to the beginning of your sentence.

- 혹시 방탄소년단 알아요?
  By any chance, do you know BTS?
- 혹시 저 좀 도와줄 수 있어요?
  By any chance, can you help me?

한국 사이즈 알아보기
Size Measurements Used in Korea

When you are shopping for clothes or shoes, you will find that different countries or regions have slightly different ways of labeling sizes. Knowing the most common size labels used in Korea will help you shop more efficiently.

For tops, small, medium, and large are often abbreviated to XS, S, M, L, XL, etc. but they can also be written as 85, 90, 100, 105, etc., which are based on chest measurements (cm). Like tops, bottoms are often written as M, L, etc., but they can also be written as 26, 28, 30, 32 etc., based on waist measurement (inch). Some women's clothes are labeled with sizes that are used only in Korea, such as 44, 55, 66, so trying on such clothes before buying them is recommended. As for shoes, size is measured based on the length of the foot (mm). The sizes are divided into 5 or 10 mm intervals, such as 220, 225, 230, 235, ..., 280, etc.

⟨Run BTS!⟩ EP. 70 – BTS in Toronto 2

What are the size measurements in your country or region like? Even if it is the same as the one in Korea, the actual sizes may be different, so it is best to try everything on. How about asking for your size in Korean at a Korean clothing store to find clothes that suit you perfectly?

Create Your Own Vlog

Make a vlog of yourself in a clothing store shopping for clothes.

"오늘은 쇼핑몰에 왔어요. OO하고 OO를 살 거예요. ..."

Episode 11
한국 여행
(Feat. 방탄 투어)

TRAVELING AROUND KOREA (FEAT. BTS TOUR) | KOREA VLOG

맹방해수욕장 여행

 KATE

Learning Objective
#Describe_Your_Travels   #Make_Guesses   #Ready_To_Go!

Warm-up
Question

Do you know what these photos have in common?
They were all shot in Korea. Which of these locations
would you like to visit the most? If you are traveling
to Korea, how about checking out some of the filming
locations of BTS' albums and music videos?

안녕하세요. 케이트예요! 이번 주말에 슌 씨하고 여행을 갈 거예요.
Hi, I'm Kate! I'm going to travel with Shun this weekend.

우리가 갈 곳은 바로... 맹방해수욕장! 방탄소년단이 〈Butter〉 앨범커버 사진을 찍은 곳이에요.
The place we're going to is... Maengbang Beach!
This is where BTS took the album cover photo of 〈Butter〉.

슌 씨, 우리 이제 계획 세워요. 어떻게 갈까요?
Shun, let's plan our trip. How should we get there?

제가 지도 앱에서 가는 방법을 찾아봤어요.
I looked up a way to get there using a map app.

먼저 서울에서 고속버스를 타고 동해 터미널로 가요.
First, we take an express bus from Seoul to Donghae Terminal.

거기에서 시외버스 타고 갈 수 있어요.
We can take an intercity bus from there.

좋아요. 우리 저녁은 이 식당 어때요?
Okay, great. For dinner, how about this restaurant?

후기가 정말 좋아요. 음식도 맛있고 서비스도 좋은 것 같아요.
The reviews are great.
It seems that the food is delicious and the service is good.

네. 바닷가에서 산책하고 거기에서 저녁 먹어요.
Okay. Let's go for a walk on the beach and then have dinner there.

와, 맹방해수욕장 빨리 가 보고 싶어요! 😊
Wow, I can't wait to go to Maengbang Beach!

 **Vocabulary**

교통수단 Transportation

⟡ Kate and Shun are going to take the bus to Maengbang Beach. What are some other options for transportation?

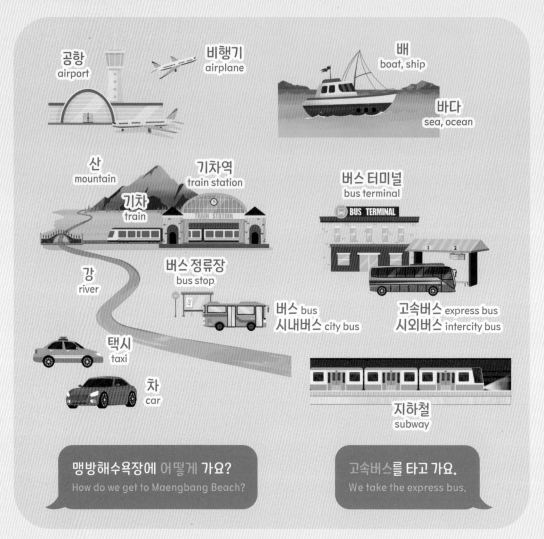

공항
airport

비행기
airplane

배
boat, ship

바다
sea, ocean

산
mountain

기차역
train station

기차
train

버스 터미널
bus terminal

BUS TERMINAL

강
river

버스 정류장
bus stop

버스 bus
시내버스 city bus

고속버스 express bus
시외버스 intercity bus

택시
taxi

차
car

지하철
subway

맹방해수욕장에 어떻게 가요?
How do we get to Maengbang Beach?

고속버스를 타고 가요.
We take the express bus.

 Practice Answer the following questions in Korean.

1. What mode of transportation do you use most often?

2. When you go on a trip or travel long distances, what mode of transportation do you prefer to take?

여행의 과정 Travel Itinerary

✧ **Let's take a look at Kate and Shun's fun day of traveling.**

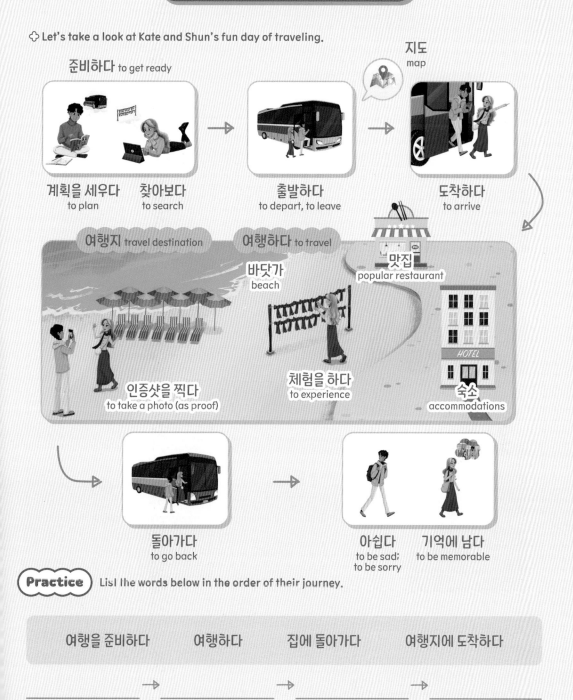

준비하다 to get ready

계획을 세우다
to plan

찾아보다
to search

출발하다
to depart, to leave

도착하다
to arrive

지도
map

여행지 travel destination

여행하다 to travel

바닷가
beach

맛집
popular restaurant

인증샷을 찍다
to take a photo (as proof)

체험을 하다
to experience

숙소
accommodations

HOTEL

돌아가다
to go back

아쉽다
to be sad;
to be sorry

기억에 남다
to be memorable

Practice List the words below in the order of their journey.

여행을 준비하다　　　여행하다　　　집에 돌아가다　　　여행지에 도착하다

_____ → _____ → _____ → _____

V verb
N noun

✦ EASY to Use!

This expression includes a verb that modifies the noun that follows. **❶** If the action already happened, use "**V**(으)ㄴ." **❷** If it is in progress, use "**V**는," and **❸** if it is expected to happen, use "**V**(으)ㄹ."

❶

with batchim before "다" (excluding "ㄹ") (e.g. 찾다) ⊕ 은 → 케이트가 **찾**은 맛집
The popular restaurant that Kate found

without batchim or with batchim "ㄹ" before "다" ("ㄹ" is dropped) (e.g. 공부하다) ⊕ ㄴ → **공부한** 책
The book that I studied

❷

either with or without batchim before "다" ("ㄹ" is dropped) (e.g. 좋아하다) ⊕ 는 → **좋아하**는 노래
A song that I like

❸

with batchim before "다" (excluding "ㄹ") (e.g. 입다) ⊕ 을 → 내일 **입**을 옷
Clothes that I will wear tomorrow

without batchim or with batchim "ㄹ" before "다" ("ㄹ" is dropped) (e.g. 타다) ⊕ ㄹ → 우리가 **탈** 버스
The bus that we will take

✦ EASY to Speak!

- 시간이 늦어서 문을 닫은 식당이 많아요.
  Since it is late, there are many restaurants that are closed.

- 우리가 예약한 숙소는 어디 있어요?
  Where are the accommodations that we reserved?

- 제가 직접 만든 요리예요.
  This is a dish that I made myself.

- 맹방해수욕장에 가는 방법을 찾아볼까요?
  Should we search for a way to get to Maengbang Beach?

- 놀이공원에서 노는 사람들이 많아요.
  There are a lot of people playing at the amusement park.

- 공원에 앉을 자리가 없어요.
  There is no place to sit in the park.

- 내일 할 일이 너무 많아요.
  I have so much work to do tomorrow.

- 우리가 살 집을 찾았어요.
  We have found a house to live in.

vocabulary

V 닫다 to close   **V** 예약하다 to reserve   • 직접 by oneself   **N** 방법 way, method   **N** 자리 place   **V** 살다 to live

1. Complete the sentences by choosing the most natural expression.

① 제가 가장　좋아하는 / 좋아할　색은 보라색이에요.

② 요즘 즐겨　보는 / 볼　드라마 있어요?

③ 어제 쇼핑몰에서　산 / 사는　옷이에요. 어때요?

④ 내일 비행기를 타요. 비행기에서　읽은 / 읽을　책을 챙길 거예요.

2. Use the given words to write what BTS is doing.

알엠 · 사진, 찍다

진 · 전화, 하다

슈가 · 노래, 부르다

제이홉 · 과자, 먹다

지민 · 음식, 만들다

뷔 · 음악, 듣다

정국 · 테니스, 치다

Example	Q. ___사진을 찍는___	사람은 누구예요?	A. 알엠이에요.
①	Q. _____	사람은 누구예요?	A. 진이에요.
②	Q. _____	사람은 누구예요?	A. 슈가예요.
③	Q. _____	사람은 누구예요?	A. 제이홉이에요.
④	Q. _____	사람은 누구예요?	A. 지민이에요.
⑤	Q. _____	사람은 누구예요?	A. 뷔예요.
⑥	Q. _____	사람은 누구예요?	A. 정국이에요.

Vocabulary

• 가장 most　Ⓥ 즐겨 보다 to enjoy watching　Ⓝ 드라마 drama　Ⓥ 챙기다 to take　Ⓝ 과자 snacks, chips
Ⓝ 음악 music

A (으)ㄴ 것 같다, V 는 것 같다

A adjective
V verb

✧ EASY to Use!

You can use this expression to guess the current state or an action.

| with batchim before "다" (excluding "ㄹ") (e.g. 좋다) | ➕ 은 것 같다 → | 서비스가 좋은 것 같아요.
The service seems to be good. |

| without batchim or with batchim "ㄹ" before "다" ("ㄹ" is dropped) (e.g. 크다, 멀다) | ➕ ㄴ 것 같다 | 큰 것 같아요.
This seems to be big.

기차역이 좀 먼 것 같아요.
The train station seems to be a bit far. |

| ends with "있다" or "없다" (e.g. 재미있다) | ➕ 는 것 같다 → | 드라마가 재미있는 것 같아요.
The drama seems to be interesting. |

- -

| either with or without batchim before "다" ("ㄹ" is dropped) (e.g. 자다) | ➕ 는 것 같다 → | 케이트 씨가 아직 자는 것 같아요.
Kate seems to be sleeping still. |

✧ EASY to Speak!

- A : 슌 씨가 요즘 바쁜 것 같아요.
  Shun seems busy these days.
- B : 그러게요. 일이 많은 것 같아요.
  Yes, I know. He seems to have a lot of work.

- 가방 안에 지갑이 없는 것 같아요.
  My wallet does not seem to be in my bag.

- 방탄소년단 콘서트가 있어서 외국인들이 한국에 많이 오는 것 같아요.
  A lot of foreigners seem to be coming to Korea because of BTS concerts.

- 슌 씨가 한국 문화를 잘 아는 것 같아요.
  Shun seems to know a lot about Korean culture.

vocabulary

N 서비스 service • 좀 a bit • 아직 still • 그러게요. Yes, I know. **N** 외국인 foreigner **N** 문화 culture

A/V (으)ㄹ 것 같다

A/V adjective or verb

⬦ EASY to Use!

You can use this expression to make predictions about the state or action of something that has not happened yet.

| with batchim before "다" (excluding "ㄹ") (e.g. 늦다) | ⊕ | 을 것 같다 | → | 조금 **늦**을 것 같아요.
I think I am going to be a little late. |

조금 **비쌀** 것 같아요.
I think it will be a bit expensive.

| without batchim or with batchim "ㄹ" before "다" ("ㄹ" is dropped) (e.g. 비싸다, 울다) | ⊕ | ㄹ 것 같다 | → |

아이가 곧 **울** 것 같아요.
I think the child will cry soon.

⬦ EASY to Speak!

- 정말 즐거웠어요. 오늘이 기억에 남을 것 같아요.
  I really enjoyed today. I think I will remember today for a long time.

- 길이 막혀서 지하철이 더 빠를 것 같아요.
  Traffic is bad, so I think the subway will be faster.

- 날씨가 흐려요. 곧 비가 올 것 같아요.
  The weather is cloudy. I think it will rain soon.

- 떡볶이가 매울 것 같아요. [ㅂ Irregular Conjugation (p. 167)]
  I think the *tteok-bo-kki* will be spicy.

- A : 케이트 씨, 저녁에 시간 있어요? 같이 영화 볼까요?
  Kate, do you have time this evening? Why don't we see a movie together?

- B : 미안해요. 다른 일이 있어서 힘들 것 같아요.
  Sorry. I have other plans, so I don't think I can.

N 아이 child　　**V** 울다 to cry　• 길이 막히다 to have bad traffic　**A** 빠르다 to be fast　**A** 흐리다 to be cloudy

• 비가 오다 to rain　**A** 힘들다 to be difficult

Practice

1. These are the reviews of the popular restaurant that Kate found. Use "Ⓐ(으)ㄴ 것 같다" and "Ⓥ는 것 같다" to make guesses about the restaurant and complete the sentences.

Example: ar** ☆☆☆☆☆
이 식당 유명해요. 꼭 가 보세요!

1: loveb** ☆☆☆☆☆
음식이 맛있고 사장님이 친절해요. 😁

2: borahae6** ☆☆☆☆☆
서비스가 괜찮아요. 추천해요~~

3: btsrecipebo** ☆☆☆☆☆
야채튀김 너무 맛있어요. 이 집 요리 잘해요! 👍

4: learnkore** ☆☆☆☆☆
반찬을 많이 줘요. 반찬도 다 맛있어요! 😋

5: sevenb** ☆☆☆☆☆
다 좋아요~ 그런데 가격이 비싸요...

6: btstravelbo** ☆☆☆☆☆
나쁘지 않아요. 닭갈비는 조금 달았어요.

Example

이 식당은 유명한 것 같아요.

❶ 사장님이 _____.

❷ 서비스가 _____.

❸ 요리를 _____.

❹ 반찬을 많이 _____.

❺ 가격이 _____.

❻ 닭갈비는 조금 _____.

Ⓐ 유명하다 to be famous • 꼭 must Ⓝ 사장님 owner Ⓝ 반찬 *ban-chan* (side dish) • 그런데 but
Ⓐ 달다 to be sweet

2. Choose the right word from the given words and use "**A/V**(으)ㄹ 것 같다" to complete the predictive sentences.

| 크다 | 재미있다 | 무겁다 | 맛있다 |

Example

옷을 입을 거예요.
그런데 옷이 _____크을 것 같아요_____ .

1

방탄소년단이 만든 음식을 먹을 거예요.
음식이 _____ .

2

제가 멜 가방이에요.
그런데 가방이 _____ .

3

방탄소년단하고 같이 게임을 할 거예요.
게임이 _____ .

3. These are Shun's travel notes. Write questions about Kate and Shun's travel itinerary, guess and write the answers, and then talk about them.

Time	아침 9시	낮 12시	낮 12시 30분	낮 1시	…
Itinerary	서울 고속버스 터미널 → 동해 터미널 (고속버스)	동해 터미널 → 맹방해수욕장 (시외버스)	맹방해수욕장 구경, 소원 리본 체험	케이트 씨가 찾은 맛집, 점심	…

Q. 케이트 씨하고 슌 씨는 몇 시에 고속버스를 **탈 것 같아요**?

Q. 케이트 씨하고 슌 씨는 맹방 해수욕장에서 뭐 **할 것 같아요**?

Q.

A. 아침 9시에 **탈 것 같아요**.

A. 맹방해수욕장을 구경하고 소원 리본 체험을 **할 것 같아요**.

A.

Vocabulary

Ⓥ 메다 to carry Ⓝ 동해 Donghae Ⓝ 구경 sightseeing Ⓝ 소원 리본 wish ribbon

Dialogue

드디어 도착했어요!
숀 씨가 계획을 잘 세워 줘서 편하게 왔어요. 고마워요.

아니에요. 😊 (looking at the ocean) 와, 바다가 너무 예뻐요.

어? 저 파라솔하고 선베드, 〈Butter〉 앨범에서 봤어요!

맞아요. 그래서 사진 찍는 사람들이 정말 많은 것 같아요.
우리도 저기에서 인증샷 찍을까요?

좋아요. 사진 찍고 저쪽에서 소원 리본 체험도 해요.

네. 그리고 케이트 씨가 찾은 그 맛집도 가요!

네! 자, 여기 보세요. 하나, 둘, 셋! (Click!)

(on the way back from the trip)

숀 씨, 오늘 정말 즐거웠어요.
너무 좋아서 앞으로 계속 생각 날 것 같아요.

그러게요. 저도 오늘이 기억에 남을 것 같아요.

- 드디어 finally
- 편하게 comfortably
- N 파라솔 parasol
- N 선베드 sun lounger
- 자 now
- 앞으로 in the future
- 계속 continuously
- 생각(이) 나다 to remember, to reminisce

Practice

1. Is there a place you have been to that stands out in your mind? Describe briefly what you did there and talk about what you thought of the place.

제가 여행 간 장소는 맹방해수욕장이에요.
거기에서 인증샷도 찍고 소원 리본 체험도 했어요.
너무 즐거워서 지금도 기억에 남아요.

2. Where would you like to go in Korea? Look up pictures and talk about what it would be like to go there in person.

향호해변에 가 보고 싶어요.
바다가 예쁠 것 같아요. 기분이 좋을 것 같아요.

I think… "좋은 것 같아요!"

Apart from when making guesses, you can also use "A (으)ㄴ 것 같다," and "V는 것 같다" to talk about your thoughts or opinions. This will make your tone softer.

- 이 옷이 더 예뻐요.
  These clothes are prettier.
  - → 이 옷이 더 예쁜 것 같아요.
    I think these clothes are prettier.
    (softer tone)
- 케이트 씨는 한국어를 잘해요.
  Kate is good at Korean.
  - → 케이트 씨는 한국어를 잘하는 것 같아요.
    I think Kate is good at Korean.
    (softer tone)

How to take a "인증샷" at your travel destination

"인증샷" is a combination of "인증" (prove) and "샷" (shot). It refers to a photo of something you have experienced, such as a place you have visited or food you have eaten. If it is a place you do not get to visit often, you should definitely take a photo. When you want to ask someone to take a photo of you, try saying the following.

- 혹시 사진 좀 찍어 주실 수 있어요?
  Do you mind taking a photo?
- 한 장만 더 찍어 주세요.
  Could you take one more photo, please?

나만의 여행 스타일 찾기
Finding My Travel Style

How much planning do you do before you go on a trip? Do you usually just book your plane tickets and accommodations and figure out what you are going to do later, or do you plan a full daily/hourly schedule ahead of time?

In the "BTS (방탄소년단) MBTI Lab 2" video, you could check out the travel styles of BTS. Jin, Jimin, V, and Jung Kook were the spontaneous type, while RM, SUGA, and j-hope were planners. RM used to be spontaneous, but after experiencing a lot of difficulties on trips, he now plans in advance to avoid this. By answering the following question, BTS got to know each other's travel styles a little better.

Q. If you were traveling with your friends, which role would you like to be in charge of?

1. planning the whole trip
2. managing funds as treasurer – RM, SUGA, Jimin
3. finding popular restaurants and cafés – RM, SUGA
4. being the head of the entertainment department – V
5. "I'm up for everything you guys do" – Jin, j-hope, Jung Kook

So, which one did you pick? Before you go on a trip, knowing your own travel style as well as that of the people you are traveling with will make your trip much more enjoyable. Which member do you have the most similar travel style to?

Make your own travel vlog including your travel plans
up to your post-travel thoughts.

"이번 주말에 여행을 갈 거예요. 제가 갈 곳은 바로 ..."

154

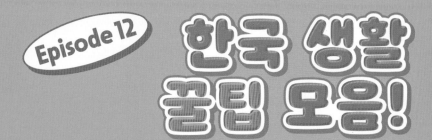

한국 생활 꿀팁 모음!

"꿀" TIPS FOR LIVING IN KOREA! | KOREA VLOG

 KATE

Learning Objective

#Life_Tips   #Make_Recommendations   #I_Will_Miss_You

Warm-up
Question

If BTS came to your hometown, what would you introduce them to? From must-try dishes, to interesting cultural traditions, to tips that only the locals know, let us know!

안녕하세요. 케이트예요! 벌써 마지막 한국 브이로그예요. 😣
Hi, I'm Kate. This is already my last vlog in Korea.

오늘은 한국 생활 꿀팁을 이야기할 거예요.
Today I'm going to talk about tips for life in Korea.

먼저, 대중교통 꿀팁이에요!
First, a public transportation tip!

서울에서는 교통카드 하나만 있으면 버스하고 지하철을 모두 이용할 수 있어요.
In Seoul, if you have one transportation card, you can use both the bus and subway.

그리고 환승 할인도 되니까, 한국에 오면 꼭 교통카드부터 사세요!
And you can also get a discount on transit, so make sure you buy a transportation card right away when you come to Korea!

음... 또, 늦은 밤에 약이 필요하면 편의점에 가 보세요.
Hmm... Also, if you need some medicine late at night, try going to a convenience store.

거기에서 감기약, 해열제 등 간단한 약을 살 수 있어요.
There you can buy simple medicine like cold medicine and fever reducers.

또 어떤 꿀팁이 있어요, 슌 씨? 우리 슌 씨 이야기도 들어 봐요!
What other tips do you have, Shun? Let's hear from Shun as well!

**Vocabulary**

계절과 날씨 Seasons and Weather

◇ Before you visit Korea, knowing the seasons and weather-related expressions will be helpful.

계절 season

봄 spring   여름 summer   가을 fall   겨울 winter

기온 temperature

°C °F

덥다
to be hot

따뜻하다
to be warm

시원하다
to be cool

춥다
to be cold

날씨 weather

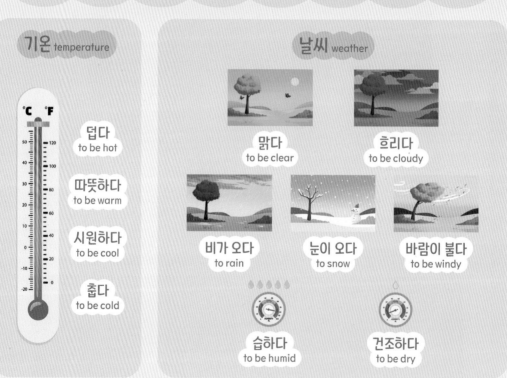

맑다
to be clear

흐리다
to be cloudy

비가 오다
to rain

눈이 오다
to snow

바람이 불다
to be windy

습하다
to be humid

건조하다
to be dry

Practice   Answer the following questions in Korean.

1. 어떤 계절을 가장 좋아해요?

2. 오늘 날씨는 어때요?

인터넷 쇼핑 Online Shopping (Internet Shopping)

✧ In Korea, you can buy most of the things you need in your everyday life online. Let's look at the words you need to know when shopping online.

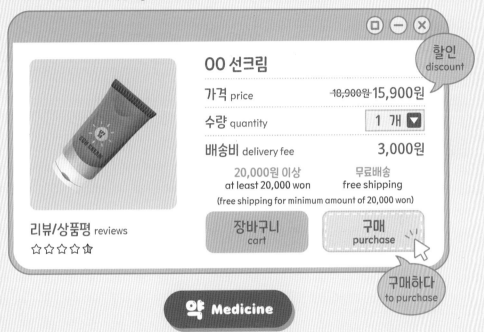

OO 선크림

가격 price   ~~18,900원~~ 15,900원

할인 discount

수량 quantity   1 개 ▼

배송비 delivery fee   3,000원

20,000원 이상
at least 20,000 won

무료배송
free shipping

(free shipping for minimum amount of 20,000 won)

리뷰/상품평 reviews
☆☆☆☆☆

장바구니
cart

구매
purchase

구매하다
to purchase

약 Medicine

✧ In case of an emergency, it is a good idea to know how to say basic symptoms as well as the names of medicine.

감기에 걸리다
to catch a cold

감기약
cold medicine

열이 나다
to have a fever

해열제
fever reducer

소화가 안 되다
to have indigestion

소화제
digestive medicine

상처가 나다
to get injured

연고   밴드
ointment   bandage

 Practice   What medicine would you need in the following situations? Answer in Korean.

❶ 감기에 걸렸어요. 열도 나요.   ❷ 밥을 너무 많이 먹었어요. 소화가 안 되는 것 같아요.

A/V (으)면

A/V adjective or verb

✧ EASY to Use!

This expression refers to a prerequisite of or assumption about the latter part of the sentence.

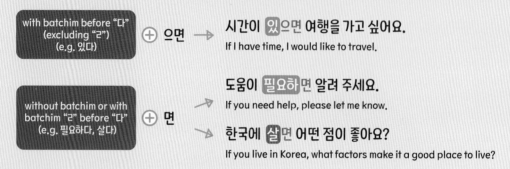

with batchim before "다" (excluding "ㄹ") (e.g. 있다)	⊕ 으면 →	시간이 **있**으면 여행을 가고 싶어요. If I have time, I would like to travel.
without batchim or with batchim "ㄹ" before "다" (e.g. 필요하다, 살다)	⊕ 면	도움이 **필요하**면 알려 주세요. If you need help, please let me know. 한국에 **살**면 어떤 점이 좋아요? If you live in Korea, what factors make it a good place to live?

✧ EASY to Speak!

- 몸이 안 좋으면 꼭 병원에 가세요.
  If you do not feel well, you must go to the clinic (hospital).

- 방탄소년단을 만나면 너무 행복할 것 같아요.
  If I met BTS, I would be so happy.

- 바람이 많이 불면 창문을 닫아 주세요.
  If it is very windy, please close the window.

- A : 좀 덥지 않아요?
    Isn't it a bit hot?

- B : 그래요? 더우면 에어컨을 켤까요?   ㅂ Irregular Conjugation (p. 167)
    Really? If it is hot, should we turn on the air conditioner?

Vocabulary

Ⓝ 도움 help　　Ⓐ 필요하다 to be needed　Ⓝ 점 factor　　Ⓝ 몸 body

• 몸이 안 좋다 to not feel well　Ⓐ 행복하다 to be happy　Ⓝ 에어컨 air conditioner　Ⓥ 켜다 to turn on

Practice

1. Choose the right word from the given words to complete the sentences.

먹다   춥다   생기다   맑다   도착하다

Example   약을 먹으면 괜찮을 거예요.

1 집에 _____ 연락해 주세요.   **2** _____ 코트를 입으세요.

3 시간이 _____ 가 보고 싶은 곳이 있어요.   **4** 날씨가 _____ 공원에 갈까요?

2. Think about your daily life full of BTS. What would you do in the following situations?

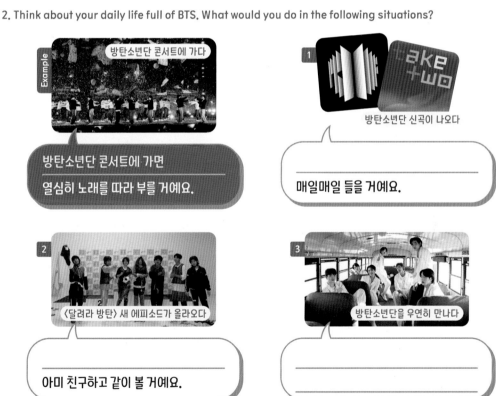

Example

방탄소년단 콘서트에 가다

방탄소년단 콘서트에 가면
열심히 노래를 따라 부를 거예요.

1

방탄소년단 신곡이 나오다

_____
매일매일 들을 거예요.

2   〈달려라 방탄〉 새 에피소드가 올라오다

_____
아미 친구하고 같이 볼 거예요.

3   방탄소년단을 우연히 만나다

_____
_____

(Write your own answer.)

V 생기다 to have, to be formed   **N** 곳 place   **V** 따라 부르다 to sing along   **N** 신곡 a new song   • 매일매일 every day

N 에피소드 episode   **V** 올라오다 to get uploaded   • 우연히 by chance

A/V (으)니까

A/V adjective or verb

✧ EASY to Use!

You can use this expression to state the reason or cause of the latter part of the sentence. The latter part that follows is usually a suggestion or request.

| with batchim before "다" (excluding "ㄹ") (e.g. 재미있다) | ⊕ 으니까 → | 한국어 수업이 재미있으니까 들어 보세요. |

Since Korean classes are fun, you should take one.

| without batchim or with batchim "ㄹ" before "다" ("ㄹ" is dropped) (e.g. 오다, 만들다) | ⊕ 니까 | 비가 오니까 우산을 챙기세요. |

Since it is raining, bring an umbrella.

음식을 같이 만드니까 더 편한 것 같아요.

Since we are preparing the food together, it is much easier.

✧ EASY to Speak!

- 시간이 없으니까 택시를 탈까요?
  Since we do not have time, should we take a taxi?

- 오늘은 바쁘니까 내일 만날까요?
  Since I am busy today, should we meet tomorrow?

- 기차가 아침에 출발했으니까 곧 도착할 거예요.
  Since the train left in the morning, it will arrive soon.

- 많이 걸으니까 발이 아파요. 〔걷다 Irregular Conjugation (p. 167)〕
  Since I walked a lot, my feet hurt.

- 추우니까 두꺼운 옷을 입으세요. 〔ㅂ Irregular Conjugation (p. 167)〕
  Since it is cold, wear heavy clothes.

- A : 우리 방학에 뭐 할까요?
  What should we do on our vacation?

- B : 방학이 기니까 한국 여행을 가면 어떨까요?
  Since our vacation is long, how about we travel to Korea?

Tip!

This expression is similar to "A/V 아/어/해서," which you learned on page 124, in that it indicates a reason or cause. But if the expression is followed by a suggestion or request, you should use "A/V (으)니까."

Vocabulary

N 발 feet   N 방학 vacation   • ... 어떨까요? how about...?

Practice

⊙ **More practice** STEP 7

1. Match the parts related to each other and complete the sentences.

| Example | 열이 나다 | • ——— • | 해열제를 드세요 | Example | 열이 나니까 해열제를 드세요. |

① 그 식당은 인기가 많다 •　　• 창문을 닫으세요　　①　_____

② 바람이 많이 불다 •　　• 이거 살까요?　　②　_____

③ 상품 리뷰가 좋다 •　　• 티켓팅을 준비하세요　　③　_____

④ 곧 팬 미팅이 있다 •　　• 지금 예약할까요?　　④　_____

2. You want to give some recommendations to a friend visiting Korea. Complete the sentences using the given words.

Example
비빔밥이 맛있다

___비빔밥이 맛있으니까___ 꼭 먹어 보세요.

1
다양한 클래스가 있다

_____ 한번 신청해 보세요.

2
셀프 사진관이 많다

_____ 거기에서 사진도 찍어 보세요.

3
향호해변이 유명하다

_____ 거기도 가 보세요.

v o c a b u l a r y

Ⓝ 상품 product　　Ⓝ 티켓팅 ticketing　　Ⓝ 팬 미팅 fan meeting　　Ⓐ 다양하다 to be varied　　Ⓝ 클래스 class

Ⓝ 셀프 사진관 self-portrait photo studio　　Ⓝ 향호해변 Hyangho Beach

🧑 숀 씨, 한국 생활 꿀팁을 들려주세요!

🧑 네. 먼저 날씨 이야기부터 시작해 볼까요? 한국은 여름에 많이 더워요.
그래서 손선풍기를 가지고 다니면 정말 좋아요.
하지만 겨울은 진짜 추우니까 롱패딩 같은 두꺼운 옷도 꼭 준비하세요.

🧑 아주 좋은 팁이에요! 또 어떤 꿀팁이 있어요?

🧑 인터넷 쇼핑이 아주 빠르고 편리하니까 꼭 이용해 보세요.
보통 오늘 물건을 사면 내일 바로 받을 수 있어요.
또 생필품부터 과일까지 모두 인터넷에서 구매할 수 있어요.

🧑 맞아요. 인터넷 쇼핑은 저도 추천해요! 또 추천하고 싶은 것 있어요?

🧑 재미있는 클래스가 정말 많아요.
특히 한국어 수업이 재미있으니까 꼭 들어 보세요!

Vocabulary

- N 생활 life
- N 꿀팁 good tip
- V 들려주다 to share, to tell
- N 이야기 story
- V 가지고 다니다 to carry around
- • 하지만 but
- N 롱패딩 long down jacket
- • 같은 like
- N 팁 tip
- • 또 also
- A 편리하다 to be convenient
- V 이용하다 to use
- N 물건 thing
- • 바로 without delay
- N 생필품 daily necessities
- N 과일 fruit

Practice

1. Below are Shun's notes on tips for living in Korea. Fill in the blanks to complete them.

날씨 꿀팁
1. 한국은 여름에 많이 더워요 . → 손선풍기를 가지고 다니면 좋아요 .
2. 겨울은 _____ . → _____ .

다른 꿀팁
3. _____ . → _____ .
4. _____ . → _____ .

2. Tell us some tips you know! It can be about anything, from cooking to Korean studies and more.

한국어 공부 꿀팁을 소개해요! 방탄소년단 노래 자주 들어요?
방탄소년단 노래에 좋은 한국어 가사가 많으니까 가사를 공부해 보세요.
〈BTS LYRICS INSIDE〉 책을 읽어 보면 더 좋아요!

Real Korean

Beginning "부터" End "까지"!

When referring to a range, use "부터" to indicate the beginning and "까지" to indicate the end.

- 7시부터 10시까지 노래방에서 놀았어요.
  We hung out at the *noraebang* from 7 to 10.

- 방탄소년단은 노래부터 춤까지
  모두 완벽해요!
  From singing to dancing,
  BTS is perfect in every way!

Tips that are sweet like honey: "꿀팁"!

"꿀팁" is a combination of the Korean word "꿀" (honey) and the English word "tip." It indicates a very useful piece of information. You can also combine "꿀" with other words to mean "very good like sweet honey" like below.

- 꿀맛: 꿀+맛 (taste)
  to be tasty like honey
- 꿀잠: 꿀+잠 (sleep)
  to have a sweet sleep (to sleep well)
- 꿀잼: 꿀+재미 (fun)
  to be very funny or entertaining

한국 식당, 이것만 알면 된다!
All You Need to Know About Korean Restaurants!

There is a saying in Korea that goes "금강산도 식후경" (Geumgang Mountain can wait until after the meal). It means that although seeing great places on your trip is important, it is even more important to eat great food. Korean restaurants will make your tummy happy during your Korea travels! Here are some tips to know before you visit a Korean restaurant.

⟨Run BTS!⟩ EP. 69 – BTS in Toronto 1

Button on the table

You will often see buttons on restaurant tables. You can press this button to order, ask for more 반찬 (ban-chan), or to call the waiter. If there is no button, you can call the waiter by saying "여기요!"

Drawer under the table

The food is here! But... where are the utensils? Keep calm and check the drawer under the table. You will most likely find spoons, chopsticks, and napkins in the table drawer!

Water and *ban-chan* are "SELF" (셀프)

In many restaurants, you will see 물은 SELF, or 반찬은 SELF written on the wall. Here, "SELF" means that it is you, and not the waiter, who has to bring certain items to the table. You can get water from the water cooler, and *ban-chan* from the self-serve area. Remember that it is considered polite to take only as much as you can finish!

Multiple ways to order

In addition to restaurants where the waiter takes your order, there are many restaurants where you have to order at kiosks or through devices at your table, so be sure to look around before you order!

Create Your Own Vlog

Make a vlog introducing your own tips.

"오늘은 OOOO 꿀팁을 이야기할 거예요. 먼저 ..."

Irregular Conjugations

When adjectives or verbs are combined with an expression, they may change according to a slightly different set of rules.

① "—" Elimination (Tip! on page 50)

| ends with "—" (all adjectives and verbs) | ⊕ | expression beginning with vowel (e.g. **A/V** 아/어/해요, **A/V** 았/었/했어요) | → | drop "—" |

아프다 + 아요 → 아파요   아프다 + 았어요 → 아팠어요
쓰다 + 어요 → 써요   쓰다 + 었어요 → 썼어요

② "듣다," "걷다" Irregular Conjugation (irregular "ㄷ") (Tip! on page 62)

| "ㄷ" batchim before "다" (some verbs) (듣다, 걷다) | ⊕ | expression beginning with vowel (e.g. **A/V** 아/어/해요, **A/V** 았/었/했어요, **A/V** (으)면) | → | ㄷ → ㄹ |

듣다 + 어요 → 들어요   듣다 + 었어요 → 들었어요   듣다 + 으면 → 들으면
걷다 + 어요 → 걸어요   걷다 + 었어요 → 걸었어요   걷다 + 으면 → 걸으면

*"ㄷ" batchim does not change for "받다," "닫다," etc.

③ "르" Irregular Conjugation (Tip! on page 88)

| "르" before "다" (most adjectives and verbs) (빠르다, 부르다, 모르다, 다르다) | ⊕ | expression beginning with vowel (e.g. **A/V** 아/어/해요, **A/V** 았/었/했어요) | → | 르 → ㄹㄹ |

빠르다 + 아요 → 빠ㄹㄹ아요 → 빨라요   빠르다 + 았어요 → 빠ㄹㄹ았어요 → 빨랐어요
부르다 + 어요 → 부ㄹㄹ어요 → 불러요   부르다 + 었어요 → 부ㄹㄹ었어요 → 불렀어요

*"르" does not change for "들르다," "따르다," etc.

④ "ㅂ" Irregular Conjugation (Tip! on page 124)

| "ㅂ" batchim before "다" (most adjectives and verbs) (가볍다, 무겁다, 덥다, 춥다, 즐겁다, 무섭다, 맵다, 두껍다) | ⊕ | expression beginning with vowel (e.g. **A/V** 아/어/해요, **A/V** 았/었/했어요, **A/V** (으)면) | → | ㅂ → 우 |

가볍다 + 어요 → 가벼우어요 → 가벼워요   덥다 + 어요 → 더우어요 → 더워요
가볍다 + 었어요 → 가벼우었어요 → 가벼웠어요   덥다 + 었어요 → 더우었어요 → 더웠어요
가볍다 + 으면 → 가벼우으면 → 가벼우면   덥다 + 으면 → 더우으면 → 더우면

*"ㅂ" batchim of "입다" and "잡다" does not change.

Course Table

Expression	Real Korean	BTS Time
N¹은/는 N²이에요/예요 N에서 왔어요	Other ways to say "안녕하세요" "No, I'm not." Negative forms	"안녕하세요. 방탄소년단입니다."
N이/가 있어요[없어요] N에 있어요[없어요]	Asking more politely Express your feelings! Thanks and apologies	집 구할 때 필요한 조건은? What Do You Look for in a Home?
N이/가 A아/어/해요 A지 않다, 안 A	Describe things more vividly! Expressions of degree What is "이건"? Using abbreviations	왓츠인마이콘서트백? 콘서트 가방 필수품 소개 What's in My Concert Bag? Concert Bag Essentials
N을/를 V아/어/해요 N에	♪Still with you♪ "N하고" "같이 해요!" Make a suggestion	방탄소년단처럼 코인 노래방 즐기기 Enjoy Coin *Noraebang* Like BTS
V(으)ㄹ까요? V(으)세요	Dine out like a local at a Korean restaurant! I like it, too! "N도"	방탄소년단이 만장일치로 주문한 '짜파구리' BTS' Unanimous Order of *Jja-pa-gu-ri*
N에서 A/V았/었/했어요	Let's do this! 파이팅! Only you, "N만"	한국의 졸업식과 수능 Korean Graduation and the College Scholastic Ability Test
V고 싶다 V아/어/해 주다	The food is pulling me in! Visit Korean cafés like a local!	K-디저트를 아시나요? Do You Know K-Desserts?
V(으)ㄹ 거예요 A/V고, V고	Talk like a native Korean speaker using omission Laugh with letters ㅋㅋㅋㅋㅋ	한복 입고 경복궁 구경하기 Visit Gyeongbokgung Palace Wearing a Hanbok
V(으)ㄹ 수 있다[없다] A/V아/어/해서	"항상" love you, ARMY The all-purpose expression "괜찮아요!"	원데이 클래스 체험하기 Taking a One-Day Class
A(으)ㄴ N V아/어/해 보다	Shop like a local in Korean clothing stores! By any chance… do you know "혹시"?	한국 사이즈 알아보기 Size Measurements Used in Korea
V(으)ㄴ, 는, (으)ㄹ N A(으)ㄴ 것 같다, V는 것 같다, A/V(으)ㄹ 것 같다	I think… "좋은 것 같아요!" How to take a "인증샷" at your travel destination	나만의 여행 스타일 찾기 Finding My Travel Style
A/V(으)면 A/V(으)니까	Beginning "부터" End "까지"! Tips that are sweet like honey: "꿀팁"!	한국 식당, 이것만 알면 된다! All You Need to Know About Korean Restaurants!

Model Answers

Learning Hangeul p. 11 Practice

1. ③ 달려라   2.

Episode 1

Vocabulary p. 25 Practice

❶ 여기   ❷ 그거   ❸ 저 사람

Expression 1 p. 27 Practice

1. ❶ 는, 예요   ❷ 는, 예요   ❸ 은, 이에요   ❹ 은, 예요

2. ❶ 한국 사람이에요   ❷ 의사예요   ❸ 방탄소년단이에요

Expression 2 p. 29 Practice

❶ 과천에서 왔어요   ❷ 대구에서 왔어요   ❸ 광주에서 왔어요

❹ 부산에서 왔어요   ❺ 대구에서 왔어요   ❻ 부산에서 왔어요

Dialogue p. 31 Practice

1. 슌. 일본에서 왔어요. / 일본 사람이에요.

3. (Example 1) 이 사람은 진이에요. 한국 사람이에요. 직업은 가수예요.
   (Example 2) 이 사람은 진이에요. 과천에서 왔어요. 진은 가수예요.

Episode 2

Vocabulary p. 37 Practice 1

1. 위

Expression 1 p. 39 Practice

1. ❶ 친구가 있어요   ❷ 침대가 있어요

   ❸ 노트북이 있어요   ❹ 지갑이 있어요

2. ❶ 티켓이 있어요   ❷ 우산이 있어요   ❸ 카메라가 있어요

Expression 2 p. 41 Practice

❶ 문 앞에 있어요 / 소파 옆에 있어요   ❷ 소파 위에 있어요

❸ 침대 아래에 있어요 / 침대 밑에 있어요

❹ 침대 위에 있어요   ❺ 창문 옆에 있어요

Dialogue p. 43 Practice

1. ② 책상 아래

2. (Example) 가방은 소파 위에 있어요. 한국어 책은 책상 위에 있어요.

Episode 3

Vocabulary

p. 48 Practice   ❶ 핸드폰   ❷ (한국어) 책

p. 49 Practice 1   ❶ 한 개 / 하나   ❷ 두 권   ❸ 일곱 명

Practice 2   ❶ 적다   ❷ 나쁘다   ❸ 크다

❹ 불편하다   ❺ 재미없다   ❻ 싸다

Expression 1 p. 51 Practice

1. ❶ 이, 좋아요   ❷ 가, 재미없어요

   ❸ 이, 친절해요   ❹ 이, 커요

2. ❶ 한국어가 재미있어요   ❷ 옷이 불편해요

   ❸ (방탄소년단) 패션이 멋져요

Expression 2 p. 53 Practice

❶ 좋지 않아요, 안 좋아요   ❷ 멀지 않아요, 안 멀어요

❸ 크지 않아요, 안 커요   ❹ 적지 않아요, 안 적어요

Dialogue p. 55 Practice

1. 안 비싸요, 시원해요

2. (Example) 이건 제 핸드크림이에요.
   향기가 너무 좋아요. 비싸지 않아요.

Episode 4

Vocabulary p. 61 Practice

1. 오전 열 시   2. 오후 여덟 시 삼십 분 / 저녁 여덟 시 반

3. 오후 열한 시 / 밤 열한 시

Expression 1 p. 63 Practice

❶ 전화를 해요   ❷ 책을 읽어요   ❸ TV를 봐요

❹ 치킨을 먹어요   ❺ 음료수를 마셔요

Expression 2 p. 65 Practice

❶ 오전 열 시에   ❷ 오후 여섯 시 십삼 분에

❸ 오후 열 시 십오 분에   ❹ 오후 열한 시에

Dialogue p. 67 Practice

1. (케이트하고) 노래방에 가요. / 케이트하고 놀아요.

2. (Example) 아침 아홉 시에 일어나요. 열 시에 회사에 가요.
낮 열두 시 반에 점심을 먹어요.

Episode 5 ·

Vocabulary

p. 72 Practice   ❶ 사천오백   ❷ 만 오천

p. 73 Practice   1. 라면, 냉면, 짜장면

2. 떡볶이, 순대, 빈대떡, 야채튀김

Expression 1 p. 75 Practice

❶ 사진을 찍을까요   ❷ 냉면을 먹을까요   ❸ 테니스를 칠까요

❹ 노래를 들을까요   ❺ 떡국을 만들까요   ❻ 책을 읽을까요

Expression 2 p. 77 Practice

1. ❶ 일어나세요   ❷ 읽으세요   ❸ 잡으세요

2. ❶ 김밥 한 줄 주세요   ❷ 치킨 세 마리 주세요

❸ 삼겹살 사 인분 주세요

Dialogue p. 79 Practice

1. 김밥 두 줄, 떡볶이 하나, 빈대떡 하나. 만 육천오백 원

2. (Example) 치킨 한 마리, 떡볶이 일 인분 주세요.
이만 삼천오백 원이에요.

Episode 6 ·

Vocabulary

p. 84 Practice   스터디 카페

p. 85 Practice   ④ 한국어를 들어요.

Expression 1 p. 87 Practice

1. ❶ 약국에서   ❷ 집에서   ❸ 카페에서

2. ❶ 영화관에서 영화를 봐요   ❷ 회사에서 일해요

❸ 식당에서 밥을 먹어요

Expression 2 p. 89 Practice

1. ❶ 먹었어요   ❷ 요리했어요   ❸ 만났어요   ❹ 불렀어요

2. ❶ 외웠어요   ❷ 피곤했어요   ❸ 쉬었어요

❹ 봤어요   ❺ 재미있었어요

Dialogue p. 91 Practice

1. 공부했어요. 〈달려라 방탄〉을 봤어요.

2. (Example) 어제 친구들하고 노래방에 갔어요. 노래방에서
방탄소년단 노래를 불렀어요. 정말 재미있었어요.

Episode 7 ·

Vocabulary p. 97 Practice

주문해요.

Expression 1 p. 99 Practice

❶ 같이 이야기하고 싶어요   ❷ 사인을 받고 싶어요

❸ 같이 노래를 부르고 싶어요   ❹ 춤을 배우고 싶어요

❺ 편지를 주고 싶어요

Expression 2 p. 101 Practice

1. ❶ 소개해 줄까요   ❷ 만들어 줬어요   ❸ 가르쳐 주세요

❹ 와 주세요

2. ❶ 들어 주세요   ❷ 기대해 주세요   ❸ 기다려 주세요

❹ 와 주세요   ❺ 사랑해 주세요

Dialogue p. 103 Practice

1. 아이스 아메리카노, 아이스 밀크티, 딸기 케이크

2. (Example) 아이스 카페라떼 하나 주세요. 얼음은 많이 넣어
주세요. 시럽은 빼 주세요. 매장에서 먹고 가요.

Episode 8

Vocabulary p. 109 Practice

1. 유월 십팔 일에 가요. 2. 유월 십삼 일이에요.

Expression 1 p. 111 Practice

1. ❶ 방탄소년단 영상을 볼 거예요 ❷ 놀이공원에서 놀 거예요

   ❸ 서점에서 책을 읽을 거예요

2. ❶ 박물관을/박물관에서 관람할 거예요

   ❷ 생일 케이크를 만들 거예요

   ❸ 방탄소년단 춤을 배울 거예요

Expression 2 p. 113 Practice

1. ❶ 노래도 부르고 응원도 했어요 ❷ 노래도 잘하고 춤도 잘 춰요

   ❸ 표를 사고 박물관에 들어가요 ❹ 축구를 하고 점심을 먹었어요

2. ❶ 넓고 ❷ 사진을/사진도 찍고

   ❸ 지하철을 타고 ❹ 저녁을 먹고

Dialogue p. 115 Practice

1. ❸ - ❹ - ❶ - ❷

2. (Example) 저는 놀이공원에 가고 싶어요. 거기에서 방탄소년단이 게임을 했어요. 저는 놀이공원에서 놀이기구도 타고 사진도 많이 찍을 거예요.

Episode 9

Warm-up Question p. 118

달려라 방탄 (Run BTS), MIC Drop, Permission to Dance

Vocabulary p. 121 Practice

❶ (Example) 즐거워요. 기뻐요. 궁금해요. 긴장돼요.

❷ (Example) 피곤해요. 힘들어요.

Expression 1 p. 123 Practice

❶ (네,) 출 수 있어요 (아니요,) 출 수 없어요

❷ (네,) 부를 수 있어요 (아니요,) 부를 수 없어요

❸ (네,) 먹을 수 있어요 (아니요,) 먹을 수 없어요

Expression 2 p. 125 Practice

1. ❶ 일이 많아서 ❷ 영화가 무서워서 ❸ 조금 피곤해서

   ❹ 한국어를 잘하고 싶어서

2. ❶ 방탄소년단 영상을 자막 없이 보고 싶어서요

   ❷ 방탄소년단 노래 가사를 잘 알고 싶어서요

Dialogue p. 127 Practice

1. 요리예요. / 요리하는 것을 좋아해요.
   (케이트하고 슌은 다음 주말에) 한국 요리 쿠킹 클래스에 가요.

2. (Example) 신청 클래스 한국어   내 수준 조금 할 수 있어요.
   배우고 싶은 이유 한국 드라마를 자막 없이 보고 싶어요.

Episode 10

Vocabulary p. 133 Practice

❶ 파란색 ❷ 운동화 / 신발 ❸ 안경

Expression 1 p. 135 Practice

1. ❶ 긴 ❷ 얇은 ❸ 두꺼운

2. (Example) 감동적인 가사, 인기 많은 아이돌

Expression 2 p. 137 Practice

1. ❶ 구경해 볼까요 ❷ 가 보고 싶어요 ❸ 읽어 보세요

   ❹ 생각해 보세요

2. ❶ 한번 신어 보세요 ❷ 한번 써 보세요

   ❸ 한번 입어 보세요

Dialogue p. 139 Practice

1. (Example) 저는 이 흰색 운동화를 신어 보고 싶어요. 색이 예뻐서 마음에 들어요.

2. (Example) 이 긴 청바지를 입어 보세요. 디자인이 멋져서 추천해 주고 싶어요.

Episode 11

Vocabulary p. 145 Practice

여행을 준비하다 – 여행지에 도착하다 – 여행하다 – 집에 돌아가다

Expression 1 p. 147 Practice

1. ❶ 좋아하는 ❷ 보는 ❸ 산 ❹ 읽을

2. ❶ 전화를 하는 ❷ 노래를 부르는 ❸ 과자를 먹는

   ❹ 음식을 만드는 ❺ 음악을 듣는 ❻ 테니스를 치는

Expression 2 pp. 150–151 Practice

1. ❶ 친절한 것 같아요 ❷ 괜찮은 것 같아요 ❸ 잘하는 것 같아요

   ❹ 주는 것 같아요 ❺ 비싼 것 같아요 ❻ 단 것 같아요

2. ❶ 맛있을 것 같아요 ❷ 무거울 것 같아요 ❸ 재미있을 것 같아요

3. (Example 1) Q. 케이트 씨하고 슌 씨는 어디에서 점심을 먹을 것 같아요?
   A. 케이트 씨가 찾은 맛집에서 먹을 것 같아요.

   (Example 2) Q. 케이트 씨하고 슌 씨는 어떻게 맹방해수욕장에 갈 것 같아요?
   A. 고속버스하고 시외버스를 타고 갈 것 같아요.

Dialogue p. 153 Practice

1. (Example) 제가 여행 간 장소는 향호해변이에요. 거기에서 인증샷도
   찍고 맛있는 점심도 먹었어요. 너무 즐거워서 또 가고 싶어요.

2. (Example) 한복을 입고 경복궁에 가 보고 싶어요. 한복이 예쁠 것 같아요.
   재미있을 것 같아요.

Episode 12 ·······························

Vocabulary p. 159 Practice

❶ 감기약, 해열제 ❷ 소화제

Expression 1 p. 161 Practice

1. ❶ 도착하면 ❷ 추우면 ❸ 생기면 ❹ 맑으면

2. ❶ 방탄소년단 신곡이 나오면

   ❷ 〈달려라 방탄〉 새 에피소드가 올라오면

Expression 2 p. 163 Practice

1. ❶ 그 식당은 인기가 많으니까 지금 예약할까요?

   ❷ 바람이 많이 부니까 창문을 닫으세요.

   ❸ 상품 리뷰가 좋으니까 이거 살까요?

   ❹ 곧 팬 미팅이 있으니까 티켓팅을 준비하세요.

2. ❶ 다양한 클래스가 있으니까 ❷ 셀프 사진관이 많으니까

   ❸ 향호해변이 유명하니까

Dialogue p. 165 Practice

1. ❷ (겨울은) 진짜 추워요 → 롱패딩 같은 두꺼운 옷도 꼭 준비하세요

   ❸ 인터넷 쇼핑이 아주 빠르고 편리해요 → 인터넷 쇼핑을 꼭
      이용해 보세요

   ❹ 한국어 수업이 재미있어요 → 한국어 수업을 꼭 들어 보세요

2. (Example) 한국 식당 꿀팁을 소개해요! 한국 식당에는 테이블에 다양한
   물건이 있어요. 수저, 티슈가 필요하면 먼저 테이블 서랍을 열어 보세요.
   직원을 부르고 싶으면 테이블 위 호출벨을 눌러 보세요. 그리고 키오스크를
   이용하는 식당도 많으니까, 키오스크가 있으면 거기에서 주문하세요!

Dialogue Translations

Episode 1 p. 30

Kate Hello. I'm Kate. What's your name?

Shun I'm Shun. Nice to meet you.

Kate Nice to meet you too. I'm from the United States. Where are you from?

Shun I'm from Japan. Oh! Kate, are you a fan of BTS?

Kate Yes, I am.

Shun Wow, I'm ARMY too. Let's be friends.

Episode 2 p. 42

Kate Oh no! I don't have my cell phone.

Shun Really? Is it not in your bag?

Kate No, it's not.

Shun Kate, what's your phone number?

Kate It's 010-0000-1234.

(Shun calls Kate, and her cell phone rings)

Shun Oh! It's under the desk.

Kate Wow! Thank you so much.

Shun No problem. But Kate, where is your Korean textbook?

Kate Oh… It's in my room.

Episode 3 p. 54

(Kate takes out her portable fan)

Shun What's that, Kate?

Kate Oh, this is a handheld fan. It's a portable fan.

Shun It has a nice design. Is it expensive?

Kate No, it isn't expensive. And it keeps me cool.

(Shun points to the photo on Kate's portable charger)

Shun Is that a photo of BTS?

Kate Yes, it is.

Shun As always, all seven of them look so cool.

Episode 4 p. 66

Kate Shun, what do you usually do in the evening?

Shun I play computer games. What do you do in the evening?

Kate I hang out with my friends. Today we're going to a *noraebang*.

Shun Wow, *noraebang*!

Kate Shun, do you like to sing?

Shun Yes, I do. I especially like to sing BTS songs.

Kate Awesome! Are you free tonight at 7 p.m.? Let's hang out. (Let's go to the *noraebang* together.)

Shun Okay, great!

Episode 5 p. 78

Kate What should we eat?

Shun How about two rolls of *gimbap* and some *tteok-bo-kki*?

Kate Okay, sounds great. Should we order mung bean pancake as well?

Shun Sure. (calls to the waiter) Excuse me!

Waiter Yes, what can I get for you?

Shun Two rolls of *gimbap*, one *tteok-bo-kki*, and one mung bean pancake, please.

(after the meal)

Kate Thanks for the great food. How much is it?

Waiter It's 16,500 won.

Episode 6 p. 90

(the morning of the test)

Shun Kate, did you study a lot for the test?

Kate Yes. I spent all day yesterday studying at the study café. Did you study a lot, too, Shun?

Shun No, I didn't study much. I only watched 〈Run BTS!〉 at home yesterday.

Kate Did you watch it too? Yesterday's episode was really funny!

Shun Oh! Did you watch 〈Run BTS!〉 at the study café as well?

Kate Well, just a little. The test is about to start. Let's do this!

Shun Yeah, we got this!

Episode 7 p. 102

(looking at the menu in a café)

Kate Shun, what would you like to drink?

Shun Umm… I'd like an iced milk tea. What are you in the mood for, Kate?

Kate I'll have an iced Americano. Let's have some strawberry cake too.

(moves to the counter)

Kate Hello. We'd like an iced Americano and an iced milk tea, please. We'd also like one strawberry cake.

Cashier Okay, that'll be 16,500 won. For here?

Shun Yes please. And please add only half of the syrup for the milk tea.

Cashier Sure, okay. Would you like the receipt?

Kate No, please throw the receipt away.

Episode 8 · p. 114

Kate   Shun, it's already Saturday! What time should we meet tomorrow?

Shun   Hmm... How's 6 p.m.? Let's have dinner together and then look around Gyeongbokgung Palace.

Kate   Okay, great! So where should we meet? How about in front of Gyeongbokgung Station Exit 4?

Shun   Yeah, sounds good. :)

Kate   Where will we rent our hanbok?

Shun   There are many hanbok rental shops near Exit 4. Let's have dinner first and then rent a hanbok there. Then we can go to Gyeongbokgung Palace.

Kate   Wow, I'm so excited and my heart is pounding. lol See you tomorrow!

Shun   Me too, ha ha. See you tomorrow!

Episode 9 · p. 126

(after learning a dance)

Shun   I really enjoyed the K-pop dance class. Do you come here often?

Kate   Yes, I like to dance, so I do come here often. What's your hobby, Shun?

Shun   I like to cook. So I often cook at home.

Kate   Wow, that's cool. I'm so curious to see what you cook!

Shun   Well, I happen to have a Korean cuisine cooking class next weekend. You should come with me!

Kate   Can I take the class too? I'm not a good cook, so I don't feel confident.

Shun   It's okay. You can do it. Trust me.

Kate   Haha, okay. You have to teach me though.

Episode 10 · p. 138

Kate   Shun, what do you think of these pants?

Shun   Wow, they suit you well.

Kate   I know, right? I like them too because this purple is pretty.

Shun   Hmm... But aren't they a little big?

Kate   Are they? Should I try one in a smaller size? (to a salesperson) Excuse me. By any chance, do you have these pants in a size small?

SP   Yes, one moment, please. I'll get a pair for you.

Kate   Thank you.
       (after buying the pants)

Kate   Now why don't we look for a jacket for you?

Shun   Yeah, great. Over there...

Kate   Oh! Shun, look at this pink dress. It's so pretty!

Shun   Oh, yes. You should try on the dress too. Ha ha.

Episode 11 · p. 152

Kate   We're finally here! You planned the trip so well that we arrived comfortably. Thanks.

Shun   No problem.
       (looking at the ocean) Wow, the ocean is so beautiful.

Kate   Oh! Those parasols and sun loungers—I recognize them from the 〈Butter〉 album!

Shun   You're right. I think that's why there are so many people taking photos. Should we take a photo there too?

Kate   Yeah, sounds good. Let's take a photo and experience the wish ribbon activity over there as well.

Shun   Okay. Then let's go to that restaurant you found!

Kate   Okay, great! Now, look over here. One, two, three! (Click!)
       (on the way back from the trip)

Kate   Shun, I had such a great time today. It was so much fun that I think I'll be thinking about it for a long time.

Shun   Yeah, I know. I also think this will be a day that I never forget.

Episode 12 · p. 164

Kate   Shun, please share some tips about living in Korea.

Shun   Okay. Why don't we start with the weather? In Korea, it's very hot in the summer. So it's really nice to carry around a handheld fan. But since it's really cold in the winter, you should bring some heavy clothing like a long down jacket.

Kate   Those are great tips! What are some other good tips?

Shun   Since online shopping is very fast and convenient, you should really try it out. If you order things today, you can usually get it tomorrow without delay. Also, you can buy everything from daily necessities to fruit online.

Kate   You're right. I really recommend online shopping, too! Is there anything else you'd like to recommend?

Shun   There are a lot of fun classes you can take. Since Korean classes are especially fun, you should try taking one too!

Publication Date	2024. 04. 05
Publisher	이충희 Lee, Choong Hee
Author	Cake Corporation
IP Content Team Lead	서수진 Seo, Su Jin
Edu Content Part Lead	이서진 Lee, Seo Jin 정희은 Jeong, Hee Eun
Project Manager	방수영 Bahng, Soo Yung
Project Assistant	조건휘 Cho, Geon Hwi
Lecture Content	최윤정 Choi, Yeun Jeong 이와이 마리 Iwai, Mari
Cake App Product	이용민 Lee, Yong Min
Cake App Content	정다운 Jung, Da Woon
Marketing	정서경 Chung, Seo Kyung
Global Biz Team Lead	정석교 Jeong, Seok Kyo
Illustration	Hosanna Arts
Design & Editing	스튜디오 온실 STUDIO ONSIL

© BIGHIT MUSIC CO., LTD. Cake Corp. All Rights Reserved.
Cake Corporation (Publication Registration May 24, 2022 No.2022-000170)
Pangyo TechONE Tower 1, Building 1, 9F, 131, Bundangnaegok-ro,
Bundang-gu, Seongnam-si, Gyeonggi-do, 13529, Korea
ISBN 979-11-90996-72-3
SET ISBN 979-11-90996-71-6

App Download

Cake is the new name of HYBE EDU.

Free language lessons updated every day!